CAREERS FOR

MYSTERY
BUFFS

& Other Snoops and Sleuths

CAREERS FOR

MYSTERY BUFFS

& Other Snoops and Sleuths

BLYTHE CAMENSON

SECOND EDITION

VGM Career Books

Chicago   New York   San Francisco   Lisbon   London   Madrid   Mexico City
Milan   New Delhi   San Juan   Seoul   Singapore   Sydney   Toronto

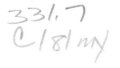

Library of Congress Cataloging-in-Publication Data

Camenson, Blythe
      Careers for mystery buffs & other snoops and sleuths / Blythe Camenson—
2nd ed.
            p.   cm. — (VGM careers for you series)
            ISBN 0-07-140896-7 (alk. paper)
            1. Detective and mystery stories—Authorship—Vocational guidance.
2. Investigative reporting—Vocational guidance.   3. Criminal investigation—
Vocational guidance.   4. Historians—Vocational guidance.   5. Scientists
—Vocational guidance.   6. Vocational guidance.   I. Title: Careers for
mystery buffs and other snoops and sleuths.   II. Title.   III. Series.

PN151.C278   2004
808.3'872—dc22   2003025813

1 2 3 4 5 6 7 8 9 0   LBM/LBM   3 2 1 0 9 8 7 6 5 4

ISBN 0-07-140896-7

McGraw-Hill books are available at special quantity discounts to use as premiums
and sales promotions, or for use in corporate training programs. For more
information, please write to the Director of Special Sales, Professional Publishing,
McGraw-Hill, Two Penn Plaza, New York, NY 10121-2298. Or contact your local
bookstore.

This book is printed on acid-free paper.

Contents

· ·

Acknowledgments

The author would like to thank the following mystery buffs for providing information about their careers:

Al Blanchard, Mystery Writers of America, President, New England Chapter, Lincoln, Massachusetts

Kent Brinkley, Landscape Architect/Garden Historian, Colonial Williamsburg, Williamsburg, Virginia

Matthew Carone, Art Gallery Owner, Fort Lauderdale, Florida

Robyn Carr, Suspense Writer, Tempe, Arizona

Carol Soret Cope, True Crime Writer, Miami, Florida

John Fleckner, Chief Archivist, National Museum of American History, Smithsonian Institution, Washington, D.C.

Connie and Jeff Gay, Producers, MurderWatch, Orlando, Florida

Noreen Grice, Operations Coordinator/Astronomer, Charles Hayden Planetarium, Museum of Science, Boston, Massachusetts

David Kaufelt, Mystery Writer, Key West, Florida

Kristin Kuckelman, Field Archaeologist, Crow Canyon Archaeological Center, Cortez, Colorado

Bob Lemons, Fire Investigator, Boca Raton, Florida

Nancy McVicar, Investigative Reporter, *Sun-Sentinel*, Fort Lauderdale, Florida

Joe Nickell, Paranormal Investigator, Committee for the
Scientific Investigation of Claims of the Paranormal
(CSICOP), Center for Inquiry, Amherst, New York

Ramesh Nyberg, Homicide Detective, Metro-Dade Police,
Miami, Florida

Adriana and Rick Rogers, President/Owners, Grace Bentley
Theatrical Productions, Inc., Carmel, New York

Al Sunshine, Investigative Reporter, WCIX, Miami, Florida

Carolyn Travers, Director of Research, Plimoth Plantation,
Plymouth, Massachusetts

CHAPTER ONE

Jobs for Mystery Buffs

Who loves a good mystery? A lot of people do, it seems. The popularity of thousands of detective books, psychological suspense thrillers, and investigative programs attests to that.

The program "Murder She Wrote" kept fans glued to their television sets on Sunday nights for years. Even a change in the time slot couldn't hurt ratings, and it still lives on in syndication. Slews of other mystery and police shows—two versions of "CSI," three versions of "Law and Order," and the Court TV channel, to name just a few—keep viewers busy trying to solve mysteries nightly.

The number of professional writers publishing mystery books each year—membership in Mystery Writers of America hovers in the thousands—seems almost equal to the number of readers. An even higher figure encompasses all those new writers striving to break in and get their first books published.

But it's not just readers, TV viewers, and writers who enjoy a good puzzle. Anyone who has ever successfully utilized deductive and analytic skills to solve a problem or find the answer to a question knows the satisfaction of a job well done. Even greater satisfaction comes from being able to combine those skills and a love of a good mystery in a rewarding, full-time career.

Do You Have What It Takes?

If you've got this book in hand, you already know you're a mystery buff. But an armchair mystery fan doesn't necessarily have all the skills needed to be out there in the field, digging, probing, researching, investigating, and solving a variety of problems.

Before we investigate career options that would appeal to mystery buffs, let's see if you have what it takes. Are any of the following statements true for you?

- You're the first to grab the Sunday crossword puzzle each week.
- You were able to track down an old friend you lost touch with years ago.
- You've done all the research on your family tree.
- You ask a lot of questions (some people think you're nosy).
- You strive to understand what makes people tick.
- The behavior of your dog or cat fascinates you.
- You love listening to gossip (but you never indulge in it yourself).
- You're curious about events around you.
- You're not satisfied until you know how and why something happened.
- You love learning something new.
- You're not afraid of acquiring a new skill (computers don't make you cringe).
- Poring through old records and dusty reference books seems like heaven to you.
- You refuse to quit until you've found the answers you're looking for.

If you were able to identify with many of these statements, then read on. In the following pages you'll find a career that lets you put your talents and interests to good use.

Investigating Career Options

Mystery buffs find careers in a variety of traditional and innovative settings. Some may be very familiar to you; others may spark ideas and give you new areas to consider. What follows is an overview of general categories. You can learn more about each career in the chapters ahead.

Whodunit?

What mystery buff wouldn't love to see his or her own creation, neatly bound in hardcover and glossy jacket, proudly displayed in a bookstore window? Is it just a dream, or could it really happen? Learn how mystery writers journey through the stages from idea to publication and how you can follow in their footsteps.

A Nose for News

Mystery buffs with a flair for words and a nose for news work at newspapers and television stations. Do you love to snoop? Could you uncover a scam? Expose a crook? Right a wrong? If so, then you could find satisfying work as an investigative reporter.

The World of Crime

Perhaps writing isn't your thing. You'd much rather be out there in the thick of it, tracking criminals and bringing them to justice. Law enforcement personnel—homicide and robbery detectives, FBI and DEA agents, and attorneys—all use their wits to solve crimes, prosecute offenders, defend clients, and see to it that the justice system works.

Assorted Snoops and Sleuths

Some mystery buffs love to solve puzzles. If this trait describes you, read about how arson and insurance investigators, private detectives, forensics specialists, and epidemiologists use their skills to find the source of a mystery, whether it is a murder, a suspicious fire, or a deadly disease.

Mysteries from the Past

Several careers are well suited to mystery buffs who love history. Historians work in a variety of settings: living history museums, universities, or libraries; historical societies; or architectural firms. Archaeologists travel to faraway sites, literally uncovering the past one grain of sand at a time. Landscape archaeologists use traditional archaeological techniques to uncover gardens that might have existed on a site in a given historical period. Genealogists act as detectives to the past, tracing missing persons and filling in the holes in family histories. Archivists provide a service to society by identifying and preserving materials with lasting value for the future. Art and antiques appraisers use various resources to determine the history and value of objects. Researchers work in living history museums to re-create period characters or to find information to help restore historic buildings.

Mysteries of Science

Mysteries of the Mind. Mystery buffs intrigued with the intricacies of the human mind can pursue a variety of psychology specialties, including abnormal, experimental, developmental, educational, and social psychology. These research psychologists study behavior, how people develop and learn, and how they react in certain situations.

Mysteries of the Universe. For some, nothing is more intriguing than the mysteries of the universe. To understand our origins they look to the heavens, to our plant life and environment, and to the depths of the oceans. They work in museums, planetariums, libraries, botanical gardens, and marine biology laboratories.

Although all these careers have distinct differences, they also have some elements in common; each professional working in any of the above-mentioned fields relies on intelligence, logic, and persistence to uncover, dig up, research, investigate, examine, probe, and explore the mysteries specific to his or her particular job.

The Qualifications You'll Need

Since the careers in which mystery buffs can exercise their investigative talents vary so greatly, it is understandable that so will the requirements and qualifications for employment. More and more professional jobs require at least a bachelor's degree. However, there are some professions highlighted here that expect applicants to have certain specialized skills rather than diplomas.

Table 1.1 lists many of the careers featured in the following pages. Pinpoint the job that interests you, then look to the right-hand columns to find the education or training requirements. Each job's prerequisites will be covered more fully in the chapters ahead.

Table 1.1. Required Education and Training

JOB TITLE	B.A./B.S.	M.A./M.S.	PH.D.	SPECIALIZED TRAINING
Writer	X			
Investigative reporter	R			
Private investigator				X
Police detective	R			R
Attorney		R	X	R
Archaeologist		R	P	X
Archivist		R	P	
Genealogist	R	X		
Epidemiologist		R	P	
Forensic scientist		R		
Astronomer		R	P	
Appraiser	R	P		P
Psychologist		R	P	
Parapsychologist	P			X

P = Preferred; R = Required; X = Recommended but not always required

. . . .

Salaries

Just as the required qualifications differ, so do salaries. How much you'll earn will depend on your work setting, your employer, your level of education and training, and also the geographic area in which you live. Throughout the following chapters, you will learn more about the specific salaries professionals in each featured career can expect to earn.

CHAPTER TWO

Whodunit?

Becoming a Mystery Writer

lthough writers come from all sorts of backgrounds and are as different as one person is from the next, they do share a few things in common. Writers love words—they love how they sound and feel and how they fit together in original and rhythmic ways. Mystery writers combine their love of words with a love of puzzles. Whereas some mystery buffs enjoy solving these puzzles, mystery writers prefer to create and build them.

Becoming a professional writer is not an easy task. The new writer faces stiff competition from experienced writers with proven track records. Impersonal rejection slips become a way of life for the new writer, who sometimes must wonder if there's a better shot at winning the lottery than getting published.

But new writers do get published every year. It takes a lot of persistence, skill, and a little luck, but if it's what you want more than anything else, you can make it happen.

Do You Have What It Takes?

Mystery writers are creative, imaginative people. They have to be; after all, they make up stories for a living. They must be able to create imaginary characters who seem real to their readers and to make up situations that readers can accept as possible.

Mystery writers have to be troublemakers, too, inventing all sorts of problems for their characters. They have to make characters' conversations and thoughts entertaining and fill their lives with action. Finally, fiction writers have to be expert problem solvers, helping their heroes find satisfying solutions to their troubles by the end of the story.

If you love to read mysteries and you find yourself stopping in the middle of a book and saying out loud, "I could do that better," then maybe you can. Here are seven tips to guide you down the road to success.

One: Don't Give Up Your Day Job—the Financial Realities of the Writing Profession

Few new fiction writers have the luxury of working at their craft full-time. Most need to maintain some other sort of employment to help pay the bills until they are able to support themselves through their writing.

Even if you manage to break in and sell your first novel, you should expect to receive an advance of about $5,000. The six-figure advances that some superstar authors receive are not the norm. Senior editor John Scognamigho says, "That kind of stuff like with John Grisham doesn't really have anything to do with the rest of us. There are 110,000 new titles a year, and there are only fifteen on the *New York Times* bestseller list at a time. Most of the rest of us are going to make a moderate income and do a civilized business if we work very, very hard. There's not that much room at the top. And there isn't much of a middle class in publishing. You either make a little bit of money, which the grand majority will do, or you make a lot."

If you do manage to land that first book contract, you will receive an advance against royalties. A royalty is a percentage, usually 6 to 10 percent, of the money your book earns in sales. The advance is usually paid half on signing the contract and half on deliverance and acceptance of the final manuscript.

Two: Read, Read, Read

If you want to write mysteries, you have to be completely familiar with the genre. You can't just decide to take a chance at writing mysteries because they are popular and sell well. If you don't know the category, including all the rules and all the ins and outs, it will show in your writing.

Literary agent Nancy Yost advises new writers to read, read, and read some more: "It's important to read other writers, and to know what other people are reading. The best writers are avid readers."

Agent Pesha Rubenstein adds to that advice. "Read a lot, but not just the established writers, such as Danielle Steel or Stephen King. Read everything current; read the new authors being put out now. This is the kind of material publishers are looking for."

Three: Know the Market

This can best be accomplished by reading, as described above. You have to know what's out there: what's being published, what's being read. Although you want your book to be fresh and original, it can't veer so far from the established norm that no publisher will want to take a chance with it.

"Know the market," says editor Frank Walgren. "Know what publishers are looking for before you go about submitting anything—before you even go about writing anything."

Four: Make the Time to Write

Dedicated writers use every spare minute they have to work on their books or stories. John Grisham, for example, wrote a good deal of *The Firm* on yellow legal pads while taking the train to and from work as a full-time attorney in a law firm.

Others get up an hour earlier, stay up an hour later, turn down invitations to parties or other social events, or let the housework go—whatever they can do to find the time to write.

Successful authors who support themselves through their writing treat it as a full-time job. Most report learning how to discipline themselves to put in a certain number of hours each day.

Every writer chooses a schedule that is personally most comfortable. Some work in the early hours of the morning, take afternoon naps, and then go back to the computer in the evenings.

Others write for eight or ten or twelve hours straight each day for months until the book is finished. Still others might take years to complete one volume.

There is no set formula for how a writer should work. The only rule is that you have to write. Author James Clavell said that even if you write only one page every day for a year, at the end of that time, you'll have 365 pages. And that's a good-sized book.

Five: Hone Your Craft

How do you learn to write or improve your writing skills? Again, you must read. But as you're reading, don your detective's cap. Look at how the author has constructed the story. See how the plot twists and turns and how it all ties together in the end. Examine the characters, study the dialogue, figure out what keeps you turning the pages. Then try to re-create that.

But you can't write in a vacuum. All writers need feedback. Many successful authors started out by participating in small writers' groups, meeting weekly and critiquing each other's work. Others attend seminars and workshops or take writing classes.

Six: Know How to Submit Your Work

Writing a mystery novel is only half the battle. The next hurdle is knowing how to submit your work for publication. Your manuscript must be typed in a format acceptable to an editor. *Writer's Market,* an annual publication from Writer's Digest Books, offers valuable information on all aspects of manuscript preparation and submission.

In the past, a novice author could submit a manuscript directly to an editor, in hopes that the editor would read the book and buy it. The writer could represent himself or herself in contract negotiations or use the sale to get an agent. Times have changed, however. Editors no longer have the time to read books that come in "over the transom." If a publisher does accept such submissions, it is possible that they are read by less experienced assistants rather than by editors. Some small presses do still consider work submitted directly by an author, but if you are interested in submitting your manuscript to a major publisher, you will almost definitely need an agent.

It is important to note that many publishers no longer accept unsolicited manuscripts or those that are not sent through an agent. Submission by an agent offers an implicit statement that the book has been read and judged good enough to consider for publication. An agent should also know which editor is the best choice for your work. *Writer's Market* and the Association of Authors' Representatives both offer helpful tips for finding an agent.

An agent typically receives a commission of fifteen percent of the book sale. While this might seem like a high percentage to a fledgling writer, bear in mind that an agent is also experienced in negotiating contracts and will probably get you a much better deal than you would be able to negotiate on your own.

Seven: Keep Writing

After the query letters and sample chapters are in the mail, many new writers just sit back and wait for responses. The smart writer puts that manuscript out of mind and gets to work on the next one. And the next one. And the next one.

In the end, the key to getting published can be summed up in one word: persistence.

John Grisham—a Success Story

John Grisham is an attorney turned writer. With fifteen books to his credit at the time this book was written, several of which have been made into feature films, he is able to command very impressive advances. His first four books set a record by being on the bestseller list all at the same time.

But success didn't come quickly, or easily, for the author of such bestsellers as *A Time to Kill, The Pelican Brief,* and *The Summons.* First John had difficulty finding an agent to take him on; then when he had passed that hurdle, it took his agent a year to sell his first novel. A slew of rejection notices was finally replaced by the all-important acceptance—handed to him by Bill Thompson, an editor who is not afraid of promoting a newcomer. (Thompson is the editor who gave Stephen King his chance when no one else would and published King's first novel, *Carrie*.) Thompson paid John $15,000 for *A Time to Kill*. It came out in June 1989 with a print run of five thousand. "I bought a thousand, and another thousand were sitting in a warehouse, so you know not many were out there," John said in an interview in *Publishers Weekly*.

Events progressed more rapidly with his second book, *The Firm*. A copy of his manuscript landed in the hands of Hollywood, and Paramount paid John $600,000 for the movie rights. And this was before a publisher had even seen the manuscript! Doubleday, one of the many houses that had passed on his first novel, then jumped at the chance to publish the book. "I still have the rejection letter," John said with a hint of a smile.

And he has a lot to be smiling about. More than sixty million copies of his books are now in print, and his novels have been translated into twenty-nine languages.

Novelist Robyn Carr

Robyn Carr published twelve books in the 1980s, most in the historical romance or category romance genre. In 1992 she changed focus, and her next book, *Mind Tryst*, a psychological suspense/woman-in-jeopardy thriller, was published by St. Martin's Press. Robyn also taught for the Writer's Digest School of Writing and is the author of *Practical Tips for Writing Popular Fiction* (Writer's Digest Books).

A Writer's Beginning

Robyn Carr describes her start as a writer as rather unexceptional: "I'm a very ordinary person. While I was pregnant, I read a lot and thought anybody with half a brain could do this, which is how everyone thinks in the beginning. You write that first book and you're sure it's going to be *Gone with the Wind,* but it's really junk. But something happens to you when you're doing it. It held my interest to the point that it became an obsessive desire to write. I couldn't wait to get back to it."

From Romance to Mystery

Robyn decided to switch from writing romance novels after feeling that "I was getting burned out. It was hard to find anything new. . . . But I'm not tired of suspense—it's like traveling . . . and who knows where I'll go next."

Constructing the plot is very important in a suspense novel, especially since so much rests on when certain discoveries are made. In order to build suspense, the author has to remember many details. Robyn makes plot outlines on index cards that can be lain out on a table and moved around. This helps her to arrange elements of the plot and to decide when to introduce certain information to the reader. She also has other people read her manuscripts before submission to be sure that she has not left any loose ends in the plot.

Many of us, both avid readers and aspiring authors, wonder about the writing process. Does an author write the story from start to finish, prepare an outline from which to flesh out the plot, or continually revise throughout the writing process? Robyn's advice, which is shared by many professional writers, is to outline, write the story through, and then revise.

Robyn always has a clear idea of what will happen in her books before she begins writing. Some minor details might change along the way, but the basic premise remains solid. Her characters' personalities, however, evolve during the writing process, developing fully as she feels more comfortable giving them specific attributes and emotions. It is usually not until she has completed a novel that Robyn is really clear on just what her characters' personalities are.

Robyn made several manuscript submissions on her own, but her first sale was through an agent. The agent sent her manuscript to thirteen publishers, and after twelve rejections, Little, Brown and Company bought the novel, *Chelynne,* which was published in 1980.

Advice from a Professional

Robyn offers a few tips for writing suspense novels:

- Don't confuse building suspense with withholding information. The opposite is true; the more information you give, the more suspense you build.
- Keeping secrets from the reader breaks a hard-and-fast rule. The reader has to know everything the main character knows. The character, from whose point the story is told, can't hide thoughts from the reader.
- Remember that the reader is entitled to an equal opportunity to solve the mystery along with your characters.

Mystery Writer David Kaufelt

David Kaufelt is an award-winning novelist and the founder of the annual Key West Literary Seminar. His work includes a series of three mystery novels set in Sag Harbor, New York, featuring realtor/detective Wynsome Lewis: *The Fat Boy Murders, The Winter Woman Murders,* and *Ruthless Realtor Murders.* David's first novel, *Six Months with an Older Woman,* was made into a television film.

David's first career was in advertising. He asked his boss, who was a novelist, how he came up with ideas for his books. David's boss suggested that he find an old novel that he loved and use the plot as a basis for his own book. Following this advice, he reworked the plot of his favorite novel, *Cheri,* by Colette, making it a contemporary story set in New York. He wrote the novel over a summer, between writing commercials, and sent the finished manuscript to an agent. David says that the agent's response is "engraved in my heart, as you can imagine: 'Dear Mr. Kaufelt, I can't do a thing with this, and neither can you.'" Despite this disheartening beginning, the novel was eventually sold by another agent in 1971.

David published three more novels before a friend suggested that he write a mystery. This made sense to David, an avid reader of mysteries since childhood. As a fan of Agatha Christie, P. D. James, and Jane Austen, David enjoys the social commentary of English mysteries. In the Wynsome Lewis novels, he wrote what he calls "little comedies about society."

Advice from a Professional

David shares some tips for aspiring writers:

- Writing as a craft is hard work; practice is what makes a writer's work improve. Inspiration is good, but you shouldn't wait for it to strike. Inspiration is not necessarily what produces good writing—practice is.
- Writing is not an easy job, and it requires a great deal of self-discipline. This is especially true if you are working at another profession while writing a novel, because you need to establish a writing schedule and stay with it.
- Have a second person read your work, preferably someone who is a professional writer or editor. For the fledgling author, a writers' workshop can provide the opportunity for this type of feedback.

True Crime Writer Carol Soret Cope

When writing mysteries, you are limited only by your imagination. When writing true crime, you are bound by natural restraints: you are limited by the facts, by what actually happened. Occasionally, an author can take liberal license, as Truman Capote did with *In Cold Blood,* which he contended was "a nonfiction novel." For the most part, though, you must stick to the true course of events.

The trick is in having your true crime book read just the way a mystery novel would. All the same elements must be present: suspense, conflict, character, and a fast pace. But you can't let yourself get too bogged down with the evidentiary material. You have to know how to structure your book, where to put what, and how to keep it interesting.

Carol Soret Cope is author of *In the Fast Lane* (Simon & Schuster, hardcover; St. Martin's Press, paperback), an account of the 1986 murder of wealthy Miami resident Stanley Cohen. Joyce Cohen, his fourth wife, was charged with the crime and was later convicted.

The Cohen family was very prominent in Miami. Stanley Cohen owned a successful construction company and had many friends and associates there. His daughter was a TV news anchor on Miami's NBC affiliate, and his wife was a well-known socialite. The Cohens owned a yacht and an airplane and had a vacation ranch in Colorado. To many, they represented the epitome of the good life.

As a mediation lawyer in a Miami firm, Carol Soret Cope drove past the Cohen house every day on her way to work, unaware of who lived in the interesting older house in an affluent suburb. One morning Carol saw crime scene tape around the house, which was also surrounded by emergency vehicles and television news vans. She later learned that Stanley Cohen had been murdered in his home.

Carol had a long-standing interest in writing. As a former English teacher and avid reader of such true-crime authors as Ann Rule, she knew she wanted to try her hand at writing a book, and she knew that the Stanley Cohen case was the story she wanted to tell. "I wanted to write about the Stanley Cohen case, but I didn't know where to start or what to do," Carol recalls. "I kept an eye on the case to see if it would develop to the point where there would be enough to make a book out of. That took several years."

Carol waited until Joyce Cohen had been arrested for her husband's murder. She realized that an arrest was vital to the story, which would otherwise be an unsolved crime and thus a less compelling tale. A friend who was a professional writer advised Carol to gather enough information to write a book proposal and to get an agent. Carol found much help in the Writer's Digest how-to books, and eventually she wrote a twenty-page book proposal.

Carol's agent negotiated a contract with Simon & Schuster. Carol received a substantial advance, and the book sold well, staying on the regional bestseller list for five weeks.

Advice from a Professional

Writing and marketing a book about a true-crime case involves specific research and a good deal of time. Carol has some tips for anyone interested in trying this type of writing.

- You can't do too much research before the trial. Look for a story that gets major news coverage and attend the trial every day. This lets you see all the characters from the perspectives of both the prosecution and the defense.
- Try to interview witnesses after they testify; it is unlikely that any will want to talk to you before then. Introduce yourself to a witness right after testimony and ask if he or she is willing to talk with you when the trial is over. Many people will want to discuss the case once a verdict has been delivered.
- Protect yourself against charges of libel. Rely on sworn statements, court testimony, depositions given under oath. In this way, it would be difficult for a witness to say later that events did not occur as you wrote them or that you have misquoted someone. Your publisher will most likely have your manuscript read by a libel lawyer to be certain that the book is free of libel.

The Future of True Crime Writing

True crime is not an easy field to break into. There are a few well-established writers, such as Ann Rule and Joe McGinniss, who have loyal followings and seem able to write about any case they choose. Their skill can make a relatively unknown case notorious based on book sales alone.

Highly publicized cases—such as the JonBenet Ramsey murder, the Washington, D.C., sniper case, or the O. J. Simpson trial— often spawn a wealth of books by various authors. Well-known cases such as these are sometimes the way for a novice writer to find some success. People associated with the case, from police detectives to associates of the victim or the accused, often try to publish their personal take on the crime. In addition, journalists sometimes become interested in a particular case and publish their research in a true crime book.

However, the tremendous number of books generated by such famous cases means that some, although published, will go largely unnoticed. More than fifty books were written about the O. J. Simpson trial; it is very likely that some did not do well.

Since so many of the big national stories are written about so extensively, Carol Soret Cope recommends looking for more regional material: "Concentrate on stories that have the usual elements—intrigue, sex, murder, and maybe a macabre element."

Readers who genuinely like true crime stories might be drawn to a lesser-known case, if the tale is told well. A good agent should be able to guide a new writer through preparing a proposal and finding a suitable publisher.

Organizations for Mystery Writers

Mystery writers benefit greatly from getting together to talk plot and strategy and give feedback to one another on their writing.

Mystery Writers of America

Mystery Writers of America (MWA), founded in 1945, is a professional writers' association dedicated to mystery, crime, and suspense writing. Past presidents include Sue Grafton, Elmore Leonard, Mary Higgins Clark, Gregory McDonald, Phyllis

Whitney, and Raymond Chandler. There are four categories of membership:

- **Active members** are published professional writers of fiction or nonfiction in the mystery, crime, or suspense field who live in the United States. Only active members may vote or hold office.
- **Associate members** are professionals active in the mystery or crime-writing field in a capacity other than creative writing, such as reporters, critics, agents, publicists, librarians, booksellers, law enforcement personnel, and private investigators.
- **Affiliate members** are people who are interested in the mystery or crime-writing field or who aspire to write in the field.
- **Corresponding members** are active or interested in the mystery or crime-writing field and live outside of the United States.

The national office is located in New York, and at this writing, there are ten regional chapters serving all parts of the country. Membership fees are paid annually to the national office and cover membership in a local chapter. To find the address of the local chapter nearest you, contact the national office, whose address is listed at the end of the chapter.

Besides keeping all the local chapters together, the national office is basically a watchdog of legislation and tax situations that affect writers. It is allied with the Authors Guild and other similar professional organizations. At the heart of the organization is the interest of the professional writer.

The national office maintains an extensive library of reference materials and critical studies in the mystery, crime, and suspense fields. Some MWA members are well known in the fields of criminology and crime investigation, and if a member needs source material, a phone call to "national" will point him or her in the right direction. In addition, the MWA website offers extensive information for writers, including such topics as useful books, lists of mystery bookstores, and research and reference sources. There are also links about the business of writing, from finding an agent to contracts to electronic rights. In addition, MWA puts out an anthology every few years, a collection of the work of esteemed members.

MWA awards the Edgar Allan Poe Award (the Edgar) for excellence in mystery, crime, and suspense writing and the Grand Master Award for lifetime achievement. The first Grand Master recipient was Agatha Christie; other recipients have included Mickey Spillane, Lawrence Block, Tony Hillerman, and John D. MacDonald.

A Look at a Local MWA Chapter. Al Blanchard is currently serving his second term as president of the New England chapter of Mystery Writers of America. He is the author of the Steve Asher and James Callahan mystery series and has just published a new novel, *The Disappearance of Jenna Drago* (Koenisha Publications).

According to Al, the goal of the chapter is to encourage writing and to provide an opportunity for both published and unpublished writers to network and share their work with other writers. The chapter holds monthly meetings from October to June and welcomes nonmembers, who can attend as a way of deciding whether mystery writing is right for them.

Each monthly meeting includes a guest speaker, often a homicide detective or someone who works in forensics. The chapter publishes a monthly newsletter, *The Semi-Private Eye*, that summarizes the meeting for members who could not attend. The newsletter also announces member achievements, such as the publication of a new book. Members also receive *The Third Degree*, the MWA newsletter that is published ten times a year.

In addition to meetings, Al Blanchard organizes panels at bookstores and libraries. Both published and unpublished writers can read their work at the panels, which provide another opportunity for communication among writers in the area. The chapter also participates in workshops with the organization Sisters in Crime.

Every autumn the chapter holds its New England Crime Bake, a two-day event for members. As Al describes it, the first day includes mystery writers on panels talking about the craft of writing. Discussions include topics such as how to break into the field and how to improve your writing. Day two is what Al calls "the reality of mystery writing." In this session, professionals such as police detectives and psychologists give talks on topics of interest to mystery authors.

Most local chapters host events similar to the Crime Bake. The Midwest chapter has a one-day event called Of Dark and Stormy Nights, and the Northern California chapter holds Mystery Week. Contact the national office of MWA or visit the website for a list of regional chapters and upcoming events.

Not all members of the New England chapter are professional authors. Of the 130 members in New England, some are librarians and bookstore owners, and some are unpublished writers. All of the writers in the chapter are fiction writers.

Sisters in Crime

Sisters in Crime was organized in 1986 by some female mystery writers who were aware that although women were writing nearly half of the mysteries in the country, they were getting only about fifteen percent of the reviews. The purpose of Sisters in Crime is to create a level playing field for women who write mysteries.

Members of this international organization include authors, agents, booksellers, editors, librarians, critics, and readers. Men are welcome to join. According to the organization's website, membership is 3,600 and growing. Of current members, 939 are published mystery writers and 472 are published in other fields.

Sisters in Crime has forty-six local chapters, including chapters in Canada, Germany, and Australia, and an Internet chapter. Local chapters offer programs on the writing craft, law enforcement, and forensic science. Chapters also offer authors' talks, panels, and writing programs to schools, local organizations, and libraries.

Sisters in Crime publishes a national newsletter, *InSinC*, four times a year. It covers upcoming events, news about members, and articles of interest to writers. There are also in-house publications to which members have access.

For more information, contact the national office of Sisters in Crime in Lawrence, Kansas. The contact information is listed at the end of this chapter.

Crime Writers of Canada

Crime Writers of Canada is a national organization for Canadian crime writers, associated professionals, and anyone else with a serious interest in Canadian crime writing. Its mission is to promote Canadian crime writing and to raise the profile of Canadian crime writers from coast to coast.

Crime Writers of Canada publishes a quarterly newsletter, *Fingerprints*, and a directory of members' books called *In Cold Blood*. The organization presents the annual Arthur Ellis Awards, Canada's national awards in the crime-writing field.

Crime Writers of Canada has regional branches in Vancouver, Victoria, Ontario, and Montreal. There are three categories of membership:

- **Full members** who are professional authors.
- **Full members** who are publishers, editors, agents, booksellers, and others in the publishing industry.
- **Associate members** are unpublished authors, fans, librarians, and others interested in crime writing.

For More Information

Any writer needs reference books that provide helpful information. Following are a few titles that are useful to the mystery writer.

The Howdunit Writing Series from Writer's Digest Books includes twelve volumes that each address a different aspect of crimes, weapons, injuries, and investigations. The books can be purchased individually, but the entire collection is summarized in one volume:

Boertlein, John, ed. *Howdunit: Guide to How Crimes Are Committed and Solved.* Cincinnati: F & W Publications, Inc., 2000.

Other helpful resources include the following:

Campbell, Andrea. *Making Crime Pay: The Writer's Guide to Criminal Law, Evidence, and Procedure.* New York: Allworth Press, 2002.

Corvasce, Mauro V., and Joseph R. Paglino. *Modus Operandi.* Cincinnati: Writer's Digest Books, 2001.

Grafton, Sue, ed. *Writing Mysteries.* Cincinnati: Writer's Digest Books, 2002.

Newton, Michael. *The Encyclopedia of Serial Killers.* New York: Facts on File, 2000.

Ramsland, Katherine, ed. *The Criminal Mind: A Writer's Guide to Forensic Psychology.* Cincinnati: Writer's Digest Books, 2002.

Skillman, Trish Macdonald. *Writing the Thriller.* Cincinnati: Writer's Digests Books, 2000.

Information about all aspects of writing is available in:

Writer's Digest Magazine
F&W Publications, Inc.
4700 East Galbraith Road
Cincinnati, OH 45236
www.writersdigest.com

For information on finding an agent, contact:

Association of Authors' Representatives, Inc.
P.O. Box 237202, Ansonia Station
New York, NY 10003
www.aar-online.org

Literary Market Place
Information Today, Inc.
143 Old Marlton Pike
Medford, NJ 08055
www.literarymarketplace.com
    This is an annual directory and website listing publishers and agents
    in the United States and Canada.

Writers' Associations

Crime Writers of Canada
3007 Kingston Road, Box 113
Toronto, ON M1M 1P1
Canada
www.crimewriterscanada.com

Mystery Writers of America, Inc.
17 East Forty-Seventh Street, Sixth Floor
New York, NY 10017
www.mysterywriters.org

Sisters in Crime
P.O. Box 442124
Lawrence, KS 06044
www.sistersincrime.org

CHAPTER THREE

A Nose for News

D o you have a nose for news? Are you up on current events, aware of how your government operates? Would you enjoy sleuthing and snooping, uncovering scams and fraudulent practices, or breaking stories that affect the lives of others? If so, then a career as an investigative reporter might be the right path for you to take.

Investigative Reporters

People want to know what's going on around them. Just look at the popularity of TV magazine shows: "60 Minutes," "20/20," "Dateline," and "48 Hours" are just part of a full lineup on the various networks. Tabloid shows are also popular—"Inside Edition" and "Hard Copy" never seem to lack for ratings. TV news programs, from local to national, also abound. CNN, Fox News, and MSNBC broadcast news around the clock, and most cable television services have a full-day local news channel. All the different kinds of TV news and magazine programs use the services of investigative reporters. Newspapers and magazines also hire investigative reporters.

In this chapter, you will meet two investigative reporters: one who works for a major television station, the other for a large-circulation newspaper. You will learn what their jobs really entail, how they got started, and how you might embark on this interesting career path. But first, we will look at the details of getting into the journalism field.

The Job Requirements

Most organizations employing investigative reporters look for candidates with bachelor's degrees in journalism, but some hire graduates with other majors. Larger city newspapers or television stations might also look for applicants with a degree in a specialty such as economics, political science, or business. A minimum of three to five years as a reporter is also a prerequisite at large papers and stations. Experience on high school or college newspapers, local radio stations, or other news organizations is considered a plus. An internship with a news organization can also give you a foot in the door. Most newspapers, magazines, and broadcast stations offer reporting internships for students interested in journalism.

More than 400 colleges and universities in the United States offer bachelor's degree programs in journalism, and 120 schools offer master's degree programs. In Canada, six schools offer bachelor's or master's programs in journalism. Students planning careers in newspaper or magazine work usually specialize in news-editorial journalism. Those planning careers in new media, such as online newspapers or magazines, need a combination of traditional and new journalism skills. Creating a story for online presentation, for instance, involves knowing how to use computer software to combine online story text with audio and video elements and graphics.

Students interested in careers in journalism benefit by excelling in high school English, social studies, and journalism courses. Ability in a foreign language can also be useful in some jobs. Along with word-processing skills, reporters should also have some computer graphics and desktop publishing skills. Investigative reporters also use computers to analyze data; familiarity with databases and good math skills are useful here.

Career Outlook and Earnings

Most reporters begin their careers at small publications or broadcast stations as general assignment reporters or copy editors. New reporters usually cover court proceedings and civic and club meetings; with experience, they move on to more difficult assignments or specialize in a specific field. Advancement is also possible by moving to a larger news organization where more opportunities exist.

Competition is strong for jobs on large metropolitan newspapers, television stations, and national magazines. The most talented reporters have the upper hand in finding the best jobs, especially those who can handle highly specialized scientific or technical subjects. The growth of online newspapers and magazines will create more jobs for reporters.

Salaries for reporters vary widely. Median annual earnings of news analysts, reporters, and correspondents in 2000 were $29,110. The middle 50 percent earned between $21,320 and $45,540. The lowest 10 percent earned less than $16,540, and the highest 10 percent earned more than $69,300.

Working on Television: Al Sunshine

Al Sunshine is a familiar face throughout south Florida. He is perhaps best known for his "Shame on You" reports seen on WFOR, the CBS affiliate in Miami. "'Shame on You' is an investigative consumer action franchise for the station," Al explains. "We basically look at government incompetence, pollution, unscrupulous business practices, and we try to personalize the stories for people who are involved. After a lot of investigation and a lot of careful writing and production, we let people literally shake their fingers and say, 'shame on you,' to the bad guys."

Al Sunshine's career began as early as his high school days in the metropolitan New York–New Jersey area. Always curious about what was happening around him, Al started writing and taking pictures for the high school paper. He found that his curiosity went further than the events themselves; he wanted to know why things were happening. As Al describes it, he wanted to know "why some systems that were there to protect us weren't working."

Al attended the University of Miami, beginning his studies as a marine biology major. He switched to psychology and eventually to mass communications, graduating with a double major in psychology and communications.

After graduation, Al hit the ground running. He quickly escalated from covering campus news for the university paper to reporting on Watergate, Kent State, and confrontations at the 1972 Democratic and Republican conventions. In Al's words, "I cut my teeth working television on some very important issues."

Al covered many interesting stories over the next several years. He worked with WTVJ, the CBS affiliate at the time, for twelve years. He then moved to CNN, where he reported on the space shuttle *Challenger* and problems in the space program at NASA. He also covered the Contras from behind enemy lines in Nicaragua, as well as the covert airline supply operation for the Contras that was based out of south Florida. In 1989 he took over the "Shame on You" spot on CBS.

He has reported on scams against women, such as fraudulent diet and health claims, modeling agency scams, and the negative side of the modeling industry, where young girls are convinced to pay thousands of dollars with the promise of a modeling career that never happens.

Al also reported on unsanitary conditions in school cafeterias. This last report got him on Geraldo Rivera's television show. In addition, the report was shown in the Florida legislature and resulted in new disclosure laws requiring schools to post their health inspections. Al has also testified before state committees, and his investigative work has led to changes in many laws.

Perhaps the greatest impact resulted from stories Al reported on car repair fraud and scams. The stories revealed the frustration of consumers who had been cheated by unscrupulous mechanics. As a result of Al's reporting, two Florida counties now have car repair regulations, and a statewide car repair law for consumers has been instituted.

The work can be emotionally draining, even for a seasoned reporter. Many years ago Al reported on two children abducted at gunpoint from a church ice cream social. As he was interviewing the police at the site where the bodies were found, a stranger next to him collapsed in tears. The man's son was missing, and he rushed to the crime scene as soon as he heard about it on the news. It turned out that his son was one of the victims.

Despite the number of years that have passed, Al has not forgotten this story and tells it to reinforce that this is not a nine-to-five job that you can leave at the office at the end of the day. In Al's words, "You'll be dancing in and out of other people's tragedies, and it will take a toll on you."

Advice from a Professional

Al Sunshine has a few tips for the aspiring investigative reporter:

- Do not take no for an answer, whether from a prospective employer or from a potential source for a story. This is the kind of work that no one will help you with, and you must be prepared to pursue it in the face of adversity.
- Investigative reporting is almost more a lifestyle than a job. You have to be alert at all times for possible stories and be able to put others' tragedies in perspective.
- Journalism carries responsibility. Revealing a problem is not enough; you must show both sides and give your audience a perspective on why things have happened. You must offer possible solutions and ways to prevent future problems.
- The decision whether to study journalism or pursue a liberal arts education is a personal one. Remember, however, that the world does not revolve around journalism, but around family, work, education, and history. A good reporter must write well and understand economics and local government. A liberal arts education can help you become a well-rounded individual.

Working for a Newspaper: Nancy McVicar

Nancy McVicar is a senior writer at the *Sun-Sentinel,* a Fort Lauderdale, Florida, newspaper with a circulation of about one million. She works on the "Lifestyle" section, writing articles on health, medicine, and fitness. Her work has been nominated for the Pulitzer Prize, and several of her stories have won national awards.

Nancy McVicar was always interested in writing and got her start writing novels and poetry. While she still does that, it is investigative reporting that is her livelihood. Although she doesn't have any formal medical background, Nancy has many relatives in the medical field and has been interested in the area for a long time.

Nancy got her first job by answering a blind ad for "someone with a good English background." The position took her to Kansas, where she worked as assistant to the society editor of a small paper. She started out writing about weddings and engagements and later branched out, writing her own features.

Nancy also worked as an editor for seven years. She enjoyed the work, but she returned to writing because it really is her preference. As Nancy says, "I'd rather do the sleuthing that it takes to produce a story than deal with the nuts and bolts of going to meetings every day and editing other people's work. I prefer the writing; it's more creative."

Unlike some health reporters, Nancy did not know that this was the field she would ultimately work in. The job was offered after she had done many other newspaper jobs, and it seemed appealing. Health writing in particular is interesting to Nancy because the field is always changing, and there is always something new to write about. An investigative health reporter can choose what she is interested in or what she thinks will interest her readers.

Nancy explains that there is an investigative aspect to medical writing: "You may have to start from scratch, search documents, knock on doors." Nancy wrote an investigative story about how

HMOs treat their Medicare-age patients. Over a six-month period, Nancy and two cowriters and investigators researched whether HMOs provide lesser quality care to patients over age sixty-five. Nancy followed up on complaints from readers who believed they or a loved one had been denied proper medical care.

This kind of investigative work can be done individually, but Nancy cautions that it moves much faster if you have help. "You may have to sift through tons of documents, which we did. We concluded that there were a lot of problems. Once we brought them to light, the federal government promised that they would fix them. They worked on it, but they haven't fixed anything yet. So my coworkers did another story, a follow-up, which brought more problems to light. And again the government is promising to make changes to protect people's lives."

The Medicare story was a five-day series that went out over the wire services and got a lot of exposure. Nancy and her two cowriters won several awards as a result of the series. As Nancy says, "It's gratifying to be a change agent: that's the whole point of an investigative piece, to get some change going."

Nancy was the first to break the story "Are Your Cellular Telephones Safe?" She produced two or three articles on the topic, and the stories went out over the wire and ended up on "20/20" and "60 Minutes." The General Accounting Office, the investigative arm of the U.S. Congress, was asked to do an in-depth report on whether cell phones are safe, based on the stories Nancy wrote.

The way Nancy became involved with this story is an example of how a mystery buff can end up finding a compelling puzzle to solve. She was writing a bigger piece on the latest treatments for brain tumors, and she kept hearing that some people believed that their cellular phones had caused their brain tumors. Although her first reaction was skepticism, Nancy started investigating, and found that it could be true. There's no proof that it is, but phone companies have started putting disclaimers in their user manuals alerting consumers to potential health risks.

Nancy also did a piece on how emergency rooms are often used in place of doctors' offices by people who don't have insurance. Her story points out that medical professionals who are trained to handle trauma are instead treating sore throats and sniffles. Nancy describes this story as "a mini-investigation. I spent time at two different hospitals observing what went on during the day and did a whole-page article with pictures that won a national award with a cash prize."

There are many experts who are willing to talk with reporters about medical stories. Nancy advises doing some background work before talking with a doctor to be sure that you ask intelligent questions and don't waste the doctor's time.

Nancy uses a number of research methods in preparing her stories. She can ask her paper's resource center for information on what has been written about a specific subject, and the results are obtained through searching an electronic database. The Internet offers many research opportunities. While preparing to interview Kristine Gebbie, the 'AIDS czar' appointed by President Clinton, Nancy posted a question on the Internet asking people in the AIDS community what information they would like to have from Dr. Gebbie. The responses provided some good suggestions for the interview, but the focus changed because Dr. Gebbie resigned before the interview took place. Nancy went ahead with the interview and feels that she ended up with an even better story about why Dr. Gebbie resigned.

Nancy also talks with doctors and other medical professionals and stays current with medical literature. She subscribes to the *Journal of the American Medical Association* and *The New England Journal of Medicine,* as well as several medical newsletters from various universities and clinics. She also reads more consumer-oriented material, such as *Consumer Reports on Health*, and some Center for Science in the Public Interest publications, including one on nutrition.

Advice from a Professional

Nancy McVicar shares some advice for aspiring investigative reporters:

- Take a combination of journalism and science and medicine courses. Some investigative health reporters even have medical degrees.
- Generally, before you could be hired at a large newspaper, you'd have to have experience at a smaller one. You can start off doing general assignments before you move on to your ideal position elsewhere.
- Investigative reporting is not work that can be done quickly. You have to use multiple sources, calling at least two or three experts, even though you might not end up quoting them all in the story.

For More Information

Information on careers in broadcast news and related scholarships and internships is available from the Radio-Television News Directors Association:

RTNDA
1600 K Street NW, Suite 700
Washington, DC 20006
www.rtnda.org

More information on a career in reporting is available from:

National Association of Broadcasters
1771 N Street NW
Washington, DC 20036
www.nab.org

Newspaper Association of America
1921 Gallows Road, Suite 600
Vienna, VA 22182
www.naa.org

For information on journalism careers in Canada, contact:

Canadian Journalism Foundation
117 Peter Street, Third Floor
Toronto, ON M5V 2G9
Canada

Canadian Association of Journalists
Algonquin College
1385 Woodroffe Avenue, B224
Ottawa, ON K2G 1V8
Canada
www.eagle.ca/caj

CHAPTER FOUR

The World of Crime

Crime doesn't pay—unless you work on the right side of the law. The world of crime offers a vast array of careers, and they all provide legitimate paychecks.

There's no room for armchair mystery buffs here, though. Any of the following careers will have you out where the action is. Some of the work is frustrating, some of it involves danger, but there's no greater reward than tracking down real criminals, prosecuting them, and seeing justice at work.

This chapter looks at a few select career paths within the world of crime prevention, detection, and prosecution from which you can choose. Read on to see what they involve and whether you have what it takes to pursue a career in law and order.

Law Enforcement

The safety of our cities, towns, borders, waterways, and highways greatly depends on the work of police officers, sheriffs, detectives, and special agents. Particularly in these times of increased national security, the field of law enforcement as a whole is more important than ever as the government strives to maintain public safety.

Job Settings in Law Enforcement

In this chapter we look at various law enforcement career options, considering the job requirements, nature of the work, availability of positions, and salaries.

Police Officers. Police work varies from one location to another, particularly when comparing small towns and large cities. Two common denominators, however, are the mission of each police department to protect its citizens and the dedication of each officer to uphold the law and to prevent and investigate crime. Regardless of the size of the town or the number of officers on the force, police departments nationwide seek highly qualified individuals who meet strict standards of employment.

People depend on police officers to protect their lives and property. In most jurisdictions, officers are expected to exercise authority when necessary, whether on or off duty. Police departments are usually organized into geographic districts, with uniformed officers assigned to patrol specific areas. Some officers specialize in specific fields, such as chemical analysis, firearms instruction, or fingerprint identification. Others work with special units, such as horseback, harbor patrol, or canine corps.

Detectives. Detectives are plainclothes investigators who gather facts and collect evidence for criminal cases. They conduct interviews, examine records, observe the activities of suspects, and participate in raids or arrests. Detectives usually specialize in a specific area of crime, such as homicide or fraud. In most instances they are assigned cases on a rotating basis and work on them until an arrest and conviction occurs or the case is dropped.

Sheriffs and Deputy Sheriffs. Sheriffs enforce the law on the county level. They are usually elected to their positions and perform duties similar to those of a local or county police chief. Sheriffs' departments are normally small, most with fewer than twenty-five sworn officers. A deputy sheriff in a larger department has duties similar to those of officers in urban police departments.

State Police Officers. State police officers (or state troopers) provide law enforcement statewide in addition to patrolling highways to enforce motor vehicle and traffic laws. They often respond to accident scenes, directing traffic, giving first aid, and calling for emergency equipment. Every state except Hawaii has a state police department.

The Job Requirements

All police work can be dangerous and stressful. Officers confront criminals, encounter violent disputes and accidents, and must be constantly alert and ready to respond to any emergency. Even with a scheduled forty-hour work week, officers must be prepared to work overtime and on holidays when necessary.

In most cities and states, civil service regulations determine the appointment of police officers. In general, candidates must be U.S. citizens and must fall within a specified age range (usually between twenty and thirty-five years of age). Many large police departments require that applicants complete up to sixty college credits by the time of appointment. After passing a written exam, applicants must meet rigorous physical and personal qualifications, including extensive character investigation and psychological testing. Physical ability tests determine strength, agility, vision, and hearing requirements.

Upon successful completion of all requirements, officers enter a training academy, usually for twelve to fourteen weeks. Training includes classroom instruction in constitutional law and civil rights, state and local laws, and accident investigation. Recruits are also trained in the use of firearms, traffic control, self-defense, first aid, and emergency response.

Police officers usually become eligible for promotion after a probationary period ranging from six months to three years. In a large department, promotion may enable an officer to become a detective or to specialize in one type of work, such as working with juveniles. Promotions within the uniformed ranks to grades such as sergeant, lieutenant, and captain are usually made according to an officer's position on a promotion list, which is determined by a combination of scores on written examinations and job performance.

Career Outlook and Earnings

A career in law enforcement is attractive to many people because of the challenges and responsibility involved in the work. Overall, employment of police and detectives is expected to increase as security issues and concern about drug-related crimes contribute to an increasing demand for police services. Job opportunities are expected to be good in local and special police departments, especially in those that offer relatively low salaries or in urban communities where the crime rate is relatively high.

Earnings for police officers vary by location and department size. In 2000, police and sheriff's patrol officers had median annual earnings of $39,790, with the lowest 10 percent earning less than $23,790 and the highest 10 percent more than $58,900. Median annual earnings in state governments were $44,400 and in local governments, $39,710. In addition, police officers often retire with pensions after twenty or twenty-five years of service, allowing them to pursue a second career while still in their forties.

A Close-Up Look at a Police Detective

Ramesh Nyberg is a homicide detective with the Metro-Dade Police Department in Miami, Florida. He started his career in 1979 as a uniformed officer and transferred to the homicide unit in 1985. Since 1992, he has worked with the cold-case squad, handling old, unsolved murders.

Ramesh believes that a police officer's greatest asset is his own ability to listen. A uniformed officer must listen carefully to a witness or suspect, paying attention to tone of voice as well as what is said. A detective conducts many interviews and must also be very thorough and try to get every possible piece of information from a witness.

Ramesh says that unlike what we see on television, it usually takes more than two detectives to solve a crime. In his experience in homicide, detectives work inside the crime scene while others canvas the neighborhood, literally knocking on every door to ask for information. As he says, "Very often people will see things, hear things, or know things but won't say a word until someone knocks on their door. Maybe a week later we'll try a block a little farther away, and we'll knock on people's doors, and a little old lady will say, 'Oh, I heard a gunshot and saw a black car leaving.' We ask her why she didn't tell anybody. Her answer: 'Nobody asked me.'"

For this reason, Ramesh states, "I don't think there's any greater weapon in a policeman's arsenal than his own ears and his ability to listen. In street police work, when you're a uniformed officer, you have to be very aware of what people are doing and saying. You can't take a report from someone without listening to them. For purposes of your own safety, you have to listen carefully to what they're saying, their tone of voice, whether it's rising or falling. I think young officers miss this a lot, but there are things people say and things they won't say that they'll only hint at, whether consciously or subconsciously. They have the potential to tell you a lot of things, but without your asking the proper questions, they won't say anything."

For the mystery buff, detective work offers the opportunity to solve a puzzle. For example, in a murder case with an unknown suspect, there is only a dead body to work with. Ramesh states that the detective must try to learn everything possible about the victim, trying to find the reasons that the person was killed as well as who would have the best motive for the murder. The detective needs to know the identities of the victim's friends, enemies, and relatives and to determine whether any of these people had a motive for murder.

Detectives on the cold-case squad try to solve murders that have long been unresolved. Ramesh says that an advantage to this type of work is that the detectives have more time to devote to each case because their work is not interrupted by a newly committed crime that requires their attention.

Solving the puzzle of a cold case often involves working backward. As Ramesh says: "Very often you start out trying to find the original witnesses, making sure they are still around. If they are all dead, there is no use in going forward. Sometimes rehashing old testimony brings out new things or things that people didn't want to talk about before. So you have to look closely at how the landscape of the people's lives has changed. Like regular homicide, skillful interviewing gives you your best chance."

New technology has helped detectives solve old crimes in recent years. Police have access to several databases that help them locate people, and the centralization of most public records and even billing information makes it easier to find required information.

Advice from a Professional

Ramesh stresses that detective work requires a certain type of personality. As he says, "you have to be flexible, tenacious, and have convictions. If you don't, then what are you doing here?" A police officer or detective must be able to put aside emotions and react appropriately to witnesses and suspects.

In summary, Ramesh Nyberg says, "Police work really involves just hard work and determination, observation, and common sense. I think that when people watch television shows about police work, they see cops as beings with some sort of special powers. And I think people who want to become police officers and do become police officers are special people in many ways, but it's simply a matter of applying yourself and being objective."

Federal Agents

In addition to local and state police departments, the federal government plays a major role in law enforcement. Several agencies, most under the purview of the Department of Justice, employ special agents to carry out the government's specialized law enforcement needs.

Job Settings for Federal Agents

Here is a look at the federal agencies involved in law enforcement. The U.S. Department of Justice oversees three areas:

Federal Bureau of Investigation (FBI). FBI agents are the government's principal investigators, enforcing over 260 statutes and conducting sensitive national security investigations. Agents conduct surveillance, monitor court-authorized wiretaps, investigate white-collar crime, and collect evidence of espionage. The FBI investigates organized crime, public corruption, fraud against the government, copyright infringement, civil rights violations, bank robberies, extortion, kidnapping, air piracy, terrorism, interstate criminal activities, drug trafficking, and other violations of federal statutes. The FBI also works with other federal, state, and local law enforcement agencies in investigating matters of joint interest and in training law enforcement officers from around the world.

U.S. Drug Enforcement Administration (DEA). DEA agents enforce laws relating to illegal drugs. The DEA is the lead agency for domestic enforcement of federal drug laws, as well as having sole responsibility for coordinating and pursuing U.S. drug investigations abroad. Agents conduct surveillance and investigations, infiltrate drug trafficking organizations, confiscate illegal drugs and arrest criminals, conduct money-laundering investigations, and testify in criminal court cases.

U.S. Marshals and Deputy Marshals. These agents protect the federal courts. Their duties include protecting the federal judiciary, transporting federal prisoners, managing seized assets, and protecting federal witnesses. Federal marshals have the widest jurisdiction of any federal agency and are involved to an extent in almost all federal law enforcement efforts. U.S. marshals also pursue and arrest federal fugitives.

The Department of Homeland Security is now responsible for two very important federal agencies:

U.S. Customs Service. Customs agents investigate cases of narcotics smuggling, money laundering, child pornography, and customs fraud and enforce the Arms Export Control Act. Agents conduct interviews and serve on joint task forces with other agencies. Investigations can involve the development and use of informants, physical and electronic surveillance, and examination of records from importers and exporters, banks, couriers, and manufacturers.

U.S. Secret Service. Secret service special agents protect the president, vice president, their immediate families, presidential candidates, former presidents, and foreign dignitaries visiting the United States. Secret service agents also investigate counterfeiting, forgery of government checks or bonds, and fraudulent use of credit cards.

The Department of the Treasury also employs federal agents:

Bureau of Alcohol, Tobacco, and Firearms (ATF). ATF agents enforce and investigate violations of federal firearms and explosives laws, as well as federal alcohol and tobacco tax regulations. These agents might one day investigate suspected illegal sales of guns and the next look into the underpayment of taxes by a liquor or cigarette manufacturer.

One agency is managed by the Department of State:

Bureau of Diplomatic Security. Special agents from this bureau are engaged in the battle against terrorism. Overseas, they advise ambassadors on all security matters and manage a complex range of security programs designed to protect personnel, facilities, and information. In the United States, they investigate passport and visa fraud, conduct personnel security investigations, issue security clearances, and protect the secretary of state and a number of foreign dignitaries. They also train civilian police and administer a counter-terrorism reward program.

Several other federal agencies employ police and special agents with sworn arrest powers and the authority to carry firearms. These agencies include the U.S. Postal Service, the Bureau of Indian Affairs, the U.S. Forest Service, the National Park Service, and federal air marshals. Other police agencies have evolved from the need for security for property and personnel. The largest such agency is the General Services Administration's Federal Protective Service, which provides security for federal workers, buildings, and property.

The Job Requirements

Understandably, federal agencies have very strict employment requirements. An applicant for appointment as an FBI agent must be a graduate of an accredited law school or a college graduate with a major in accounting, fluency in a foreign language, or three years of related full-time work experience. All new agents undergo sixteen weeks of training at the FBI academy on the U.S. Marine Corps base in Quantico, Virginia.

Applicants for special agent positions with the DEA must have a college degree and one of the following: one year of experience conducting criminal investigations, one year of graduate school, or at least a 2.95 grade point average while in college. DEA special agents undergo fourteen weeks of specialized training at the FBI Academy in Quantico, Virginia.

Special agent applicants for the Secret Service or ATF must have bachelor's degrees or a minimum of three years of related work experience. Prospective special agents undergo ten weeks of initial criminal investigation training at the Federal Law Enforcement Training Center in Glynco, Georgia, and another seventeen weeks of specialized training with their particular agencies.

Prospective customs agents must have bachelor's degrees and/or related work experience. Many agents have degrees in criminal justice, international trade and finance, foreign languages, or computer science. Prior law enforcement experience is a plus. New agents receive seventeen weeks of specialized training at the U.S. Customs law enforcement academy in Brunswick, Georgia.

Career Outlook and Earnings

Due to an increased interest in national security and the fight against terrorism, jobs in federal agencies are becoming more attractive to many people. Overall, the number of qualified candidates exceeds the number of job openings in federal law enforcement agencies, resulting in increased hiring standards and highly selective employment practices. Competition is expected to remain strong for the higher-paying jobs with federal agencies. Government spending determines the level of employment for police officers, detectives, and special agents. The number of job opportunities, therefore, can vary from year to year and from place to place.

Federal law provides special salary rates to federal employees who serve in law enforcement. Additionally, federal special agents and inspectors receive law enforcement availability pay (LEAP)—equal to 25 percent of the agent's grade and step—awarded because of the large amount of overtime that these agents are expected to work. For example, FBI agents entered federal service in 2001 on the pay scale as GS-10 employees with a base salary of $36,621, yet they earned about $45,776 a year with availability pay.

Law Enforcement in Canada

The Canadian government, like the United States, maintains several federal agencies whose goal is the protection and security of its citizens.

Job Settings in Canadian Law Enforcement

Let's take a look at the major agencies that provide law enforcement services in Canada.

Department of Justice. The Department of Justice is the largest single legal organization in Canada, employing more than two thousand lawyers from all over the country. Career opportunities at the Department of Justice include working in criminal court, civil and tax litigation, policy development, human rights law, and international law.

The Department of Justice has more than forty-five hundred employees working at the departmental headquarters in Ottawa and in some thirty other federal departments and agencies. Some employees work in the thirteen regional offices and suboffices across the country, helping the department respond effectively to regional issues.

Approximately half of the Department of Justice staff is made up of lawyers. The other half are experts in fields such as research, social sciences, and communications, as well as paralegals and support staff.

In order to be considered for a legal officer position with the Department of Justice in Canada, a candidate must meet the following criteria: be a member in good standing of the law society of one of the provinces or territories of Canada; be a member of the Chamber of Notaries in the Province of Quebec; or be an articling student whose appointment is conditional upon admission to the bar or Chamber of Notaries.

Applicants should have strong interpersonal skills, value teamwork, and have the capacity to adapt to different situations and work environments. Before an offer of employment can be made, an applicant must receive a reliability/security clearance. This may include fingerprinting and the completion of a Personal History Form.

Canadian Security Intelligence Service. The Canadian Security Intelligence Service (CSIS) is a federal agency dedicated to protecting the national security interests of Canada. The main objective of the CSIS is to investigate and report on threats to the nation's security. The agency is the government's principal advisor on matters of national security.

The core staff of the CSIS is in the intelligence officer category. Intelligence officers conduct investigations, perform research, analyze information, and prepare reports on national security–related matters. Applicants should be proficient in both official languages; knowledge of foreign languages and computer literacy are also assets. Candidates for intelligence officer must be Canadian citizens with university degrees and must be willing to relocate anywhere in Canada depending on the needs of the service.

Intelligence officers serve an initial probationary period of five years. The starting salary is $38,670, progressing to $62,240 during the probationary period, based on the successful completion of training, attaining the required experience, and on-the-job performance.

Customs and Revenue Agency. The Customs and Revenue Agency provides protection at Canada's borders, collects taxes, delivers social and economic benefits on behalf of the federal government, and administers trade agreements. In addition, the Customs and Revenue Agency monitors the movement of people and goods across Canada's land, air, and marine borders; conducts audits for large and small businesses; develops and maintains state-of-the-art information technology; and trains detector dogs and provides other special detection services.

The Customs and Revenue Agency is composed of various occupational groups, hiring employees for positions such as general services clerk, customs inspector, and real estate appraiser. Each occupational group has its own salary range; the basic annual pay rate is determined upon hiring.

Royal Canadian Mounted Police. In addition to federal agencies, the Royal Canadian Mounted Police (RCMP) provides protection to citizens of Canada. The RCMP is the Canadian national police service. The RCMP acts as a national, federal, provincial, and municipal police force, providing a total federal police service to all Canadians.

Applicants to the RCMP must meet the following requirements: be a Canadian citizen; be of good character; be proficient in either of Canada's official languages; have a Canadian secondary school diploma or its equivalent; possess a valid, unrestricted Canadian driver's license; be at least nineteen years of age at the time of acceptance; be able to pass a written aptitude test; meet rigorous physical and medical requirements; and be willing to relocate anywhere within Canada. In addition, prior to enrollment in cadet training, candidates must obtain certificates in keyboarding, or typing, and first aid.

Salaries for RCMP constables are on four levels, and the increments are not granted automatically. Officers must complete certain duties and achieve specific experience before receiving salary increases. The starting salary for a cadet is $37,267 for the first six months, or until completion of the field training program; $48,419 after completion of field training and during the first two years of service; $56,650 for the next twelve months; and $60,384 after three years.

For More Information

For information about police work in general, plus links to sites for law enforcement, government, and education, contact:

International Union of Police Associations
1421 Prince Street, Suite 400
Alexandria, VA 22314
www.iupa.org

Links to all U.S. federal agencies are available at the White House website, www.whitehouse.gov. Select the "Your Government" link, then "Agencies and Commissions."

Visit the following websites for information about Canadian law enforcement and federal agencies:

Department of Justice
www.canada.justice.gc.ca

Canadian Security Intelligence Service
www.csis-scrs.gc.ca

Customs and Revenue Agency
www.ccra-adrc.gc.ca

Royal Canadian Mounted Police
www.rcmp-grc.gc.ca

Attorneys at Law

There are two sides to every story, and in a court of law each side is represented by an attorney. Attorneys work on behalf of one or the other side: the defense or the prosecution.

Job Settings for Lawyers

For the Defense. F. Lee Bailey, Barbara Allred, and Johnny Cochran have all made names for themselves by defending high-profile clients. In reality, the work of defense attorneys is not always as exciting as what we see on televised trials. If you decide to pursue a career in criminal law, many of your clients will not be innocent, and you might not be able to defend them successfully. Some you'd even rather not represent. But in our justice system, everyone is innocent until proven guilty, and everyone is entitled to legal defense. Criminal lawyers operate their own practices, work for private law firms, or represent clients under the auspices of the public defender's office.

For the Prosecution. For every F. Lee Bailey there's a Marcia Clark. Lawyers who work for state attorneys general, prosecutors, and courts play a key role in the criminal justice system. At the federal level, attorneys investigate cases for the Department of Justice or other agencies. Also, lawyers at every government level help develop programs, draft laws, interpret legislation, establish enforcement procedures, and argue civil and criminal cases on behalf of the government.

The Job Requirements

Regardless of the setting, whether acting as advocate or prosecutor, all attorneys interpret the law and apply it to specific situations. This requires strong research and communication abilities.

Lawyers perform in-depth research into the intent of applicable laws and judicial decisions and apply the laws to the circumstances faced by the client. Although all lawyers continue to make use of conventional law libraries to prepare cases, most also supplement their search of printed sources with electronic tools that automatically search the legal literature and identify legal texts that may be relevant to a specific subject. Subscription services such as Lexis-Nexis provide access to cases, statutes, research, and analysis. Software programs exist to help lawyers coordinate their research and communicate with other professionals working on the case.

To practice law in the courts of any state or other jurisdiction in the United States, an attorney must be licensed, or admitted to the bar, under rules established by the jurisdiction's highest court. All states require that applicants for admission to the bar pass a written bar examination; most also require applicants to pass a separate written ethics exam. Federal courts and agencies set their own requirements for attorneys practicing before them.

To qualify for the bar examination in most states, an applicant usually must have a college degree and have graduated from a law school accredited by the American Bar Association (ABA) or the proper state authorities. ABA approval signifies that the law school, particularly its library and faculty, meets certain standards developed by the association to promote quality legal education.

Six states accept the study of law in a law office as qualification for taking the bar examination; only California accepts the study of law by correspondence. Several states require approval and registration of students by the state board of law examiners, either before they enter law school or during the early years of study.

The required college and law school education usually takes seven years of full-time study after high school: four years of undergraduate study followed by three years in law school. Law school applicants must have bachelor's degrees to qualify for admission. To meet the needs of students who can attend only part-time, a number of law schools have night or part-time divisions, which usually require four years of study.

The recommended course of undergraduate study for prospective law students is multidisciplinary. While there is no definitive major, courses in English, foreign languages, public speaking, government, philosophy, history, economics, mathematics, and computer science are highly desirable for law school admission.

Acceptance by most law schools depends on the applicant's ability to demonstrate an aptitude for the study of law, usually through good undergraduate grades, the Law School Admission Test (LSAT), the quality of the applicant's undergraduate school, any prior work experience, and sometimes a personal interview.

All law schools approved by the ABA require that applicants take the LSAT. Nearly all law schools require that applicants have certified transcripts sent to the Law School Data Assembly Service. This service then sends applicants' LSAT scores and their standardized records of college grades to the law schools of their choice. This service and the LSAT are administered by the Law School Admission Council.

Law school graduates receive the degree of juris doctor (J.D.) as the first professional degree. Advanced law degrees may be useful for those planning to specialize, do research, or teach. Some law students pursue joint degree programs, which generally require an additional year of study. Joint degree programs are offered in a number of areas, including law and business administration and law and public administration.

After graduation, lawyers must keep informed about legal and nonlegal developments that affect their practice. Currently, thirty-nine states and jurisdictions mandate continuing legal education (CLE). Many law schools and state and local bar associations provide continuing education courses that help lawyers stay abreast of recent developments. Some states allow CLE credits to be obtained through participation in seminars on the Internet.

Career Outlook and Earnings

Competition for jobs should continue to be strong because of the large number of students graduating from law schools each year. Increased legal action in areas such as health care, intellectual property, international law, elder law, environmental law, and sexual harassment will contribute to the demand for lawyers. Across the board, graduates with superior academic records from well-regarded law schools will have the best job opportunities.

According to the National Association for Law Placement, in 2000 the median salary of lawyers six months after graduation was $51,900. Those in private practice earned on average $80,000; those in business and industry, $60,000. Graduates pursuing judicial clerkships and working in government earned $40,000, and those working in the public interest earned $34,000.

Salaries of experienced lawyers vary widely according to the type, size, and location of their employers. Lawyers who own their own practices usually earn less than those who are partners in law firms. Many lawyers starting a new practice find that they need to work part-time in other occupations to earn supplemental income until the practice is well established.

Practicing Law in Canada

In Canada, the legal profession is a self-governing body, regulated in each province by the Law Society. The Law Society determines whether an applicant can be licensed to practice law. The basic procedure for a prospective lawyer is to graduate from an approved law school and complete the bar admission course in the province in which he or she wants to practice.

The academic prerequisite for taking the bar admission course is either graduation from a Canadian university in a common law program approved by the law society or a certificate of qualification issued by the National Committee on Accreditation. There are sixteen universities in Canada that offer law courses approved by the Law Society. A student must meet the requirements of the university in order to study law. An approved law course takes three years to complete and leads to a bachelor of laws (LL.B.) or doctor of jurisprudence (J.D.) degree.

The specific requirements for the bar admission course differ among the provinces, but in general, the course is comprised of three phases: a skills phase, a substantive/procedural phase, and an articling phase. The skills and substantive/procedural phases usually run from eight to ten weeks each. The articling phase (the development of practical legal skills under the supervision of a lawyer) can last ten to twelve months. The bar examination is taken upon successful completion of the bar admission course. All lawyers must join the Law Society in the province where they practice.

For More Information

The specific requirements for admission to the bar in a particular state or other jurisdiction can be obtained at the state capital from the clerk of the supreme court or the administrator of the state board of law examiners.

American Bar Association
Member Services
541 North Fairbanks Court
Chicago, IL 60611
www.abanet.org

Law School Admission Council
661 Penn Street
Newtown, PA 18940
www.lsac.org
  *Visit the website for information on the LSAT, Law School Data
  Assembly Service, and financial aid for law students.*

Canadian Bar Association
500-865 Carling Avenue
Ottawa, ON K1S 5S8
Canada
www.cba.org

CHAPTER FIVE

Assorted Snoops
and Sleuths

D o you enjoy solving puzzles and riddles? Do you like following leads, assembling clues, all in an effort to get to the bottom of a situation? If so, you might be interested in a career as an investigator.

Investigators work in various fields, trying to get to the bottom of mysteries that might involve arson, fraud, murder, or disease. The work is often unpredictable and can take you through mazes of clues and leads on your way to solving a case.

Here are a few types of investigative work that we look at closely in this chapter:

- Arson investigators
- Insurance investigators
- Private investigators
- Forensic scientists
- Epidemiologists

Arson Investigators

Fire investigators arrive at the scene of a fire and try to determine how it started. Although there are many types of fires, anything from a trash basket fire to a devastating forest fire, they all fall into just two categories: accidental or criminal.

An accidental fire happens unintentionally, such as when someone falls asleep smoking a cigarette or oily rags carelessly left in a corner suddenly ignite. Criminal fires are set on purpose; this is called arson and is punishable by law. Fires caused by bombs also fall under the category of criminal fires.

There are several motives for arson, including spite, revenge, anger, and fraud. The most common kind of arson fraud happens when a business is failing and the owner decides to "sell it back to the insurance company." The building is burned intentionally and the owner tries to collect the insurance.

Fire investigators check into both accidental and criminal fires. An engine company first responds to the scene and does the fire-fighting. Once the fire has been put out, the lieutenant examines it to try to understand why the fire started, information that will be included in a written report. If the loss is above $5,000 or so, or if there is a suspicion that the fire wasn't accidental, the fire investigator comes in to do a more in-depth check.

Fire investigators look at fires as big puzzles with lots of little pieces that have to be put together in order to make sense. The fire investigator likes to be at the scene when the fire is still burning, since a fire in progress can reveal a lot of information. Sometimes it's possible to tell from the color of the flame or the smoke what caused the fire. When wood burns, the smoke is dark with a brown tinge. But if you add gasoline, fire burns with a lot of black smoke. Arriving in time to watch how the fire reacts to water can also yield some clues. If the fire doesn't go right out when soaked down but instead keeps coming back, then there's a good chance a fuel was used.

Fire investigators also look at which part of a building is burning. If a house fire is burning in the living room and kitchen, for example, and then during the fire-fighting operation spreads back to the bedrooms, the investigators can get an idea where it first started and know where to focus the investigation.

After a fire is out, everything looks black, but the debris still reveals clues. Fire investigators can shovel through the mess and look for burn patterns. They can see which side of a piece of wood or what part of the carpeting is more deeply burned. They look at wiring, fuse boxes, and circuit breakers. They also talk to the fire-fighters and ask what they saw. Were the doors unlocked? Was anyone running away? Was there broken glass lying inside, or was it blown outside by the fire?

Do You Have What It Takes?

Fire investigation is not for the faint of heart. There are many dangers involved. These days, many materials in our homes are made from plastic, and plastic is made with chemicals. When the temperature cools down after a fire, fumes start escaping. Fire investigators must wear masks with filters to protect their lungs from potentially toxic fumes. Shoveling through the debris in a burned-out building is also dangerous. A fire weakens all the structure's supports, and roofs can suddenly collapse, walls can cave in, and floors can give way.

Fire investigators sometimes have to work with the police or even testify in court, so they need to have knowledge of the law and court procedure. They must also have good writing skills, since the reports they write might be read in court. And of course, they must have good speaking skills to give convincing testimony.

Fire investigators get their satisfaction from figuring out how fires started. They like to be able to look back and say that they know now that the toaster oven went bad or someone broke into the house and poured gasoline on the carpet. In the case of arson, the ultimate goal is to determine not only how the fire started, but to find the arsonist. The work can be frustrating because evidence is often destroyed in the fire, making it difficult to catch and convict the criminal.

The Job Requirements

Fire investigators must first go through regular firefighter training and serve their time as firefighters. Let's take a look at a typical set of requirements for an aspiring firefighter.

Applicants for municipal firefighting jobs generally must pass a written exam; tests of strength, physical stamina, coordination, and agility; and a medical examination that includes drug screening. Exams are usually open to those at least eighteen years of age who have a high school diploma or its equivalent. Many larger departments require up to thirty college credits or two years of satisfactory military service.

Successful candidates in large departments are generally trained for several weeks at the department's training center or academy. The recruits participate in classroom instruction and practical training, studying firefighting techniques, fire prevention, hazardous materials control, local building codes, and emergency medical procedures. They are also trained to use axes, saws, fire extinguishers, ladders, and other rescue equipment.

Opportunities for promotion usually depend on written examination results, job performance, interviews, and seniority. The line of promotion normally is to engineer, lieutenant, captain, battalion chief, assistant chief, deputy chief, then chief. Many departments require a bachelor's degree, preferably in fire science, public administration, or a related field, for promotion to positions higher than battalion chief. A master's degree is required for executive fire officer certification from the U.S. Fire Administration's National Fire Academy and for state chief officer certification.

Firefighters who want to solve the mysteries of how and why fires start can continue their training to become fire investigators. Special training academies and many colleges offer such courses as arson identification, electrical fire cause determination, forensic photography, evidence collection, canine accelerant detection training, and interviewing techniques.

Those who successfully complete their educational training can apply for certification from the National Association of Fire Investigators. In Canada, the Canadian Association of Fire Investigators administers the Canadian Certified Fire Investigator Program and provides a tri-level training course for prospective investigators.

Not all fire investigators work for fire departments, though. Some with the appropriate training and experience find work with insurance companies or private investigation firms. Private companies set their own hiring standards, but in general they look for fire investigators with proven experience. For this reason, many jobs with insurance companies and private investigation firms are filled by investigators who have previously worked for fire departments.

Career Outlook and Earnings

Because most investigators come from the ranks of firefighters, this is likely the entry-level position for aspiring fire investigators. In most areas, the number of qualified applicants exceeds the number of job openings for firefighters, a situation expected to persist in coming years. Firefighting as a profession is attractive for several reasons. The work is challenging and is generally seen as heroic, and it provides the opportunity to perform an essential public service.

Most job growth over the next several years will occur as volunteer firefighter positions are converted to paid positions or through retirement. Fire departments compete for funding with other public safety providers, which also affects hiring.

Salaries for firefighters and investigators vary according to location and size of the department. Median hourly earnings of firefighters in 2000 were $16.43. The middle 50 percent earned between $11.82 and $21.75. The lowest 10 percent earned less than $8.03, and the highest 10 percent earned more than $26.58. In 2000, the minimum annual average base salary for firefighters was $29,316, and the maximum was $39,477.

The salaries for fire investigators vary from department to department. In some departments, investigators who carry a firefighter rank would earn the same as a firefighter. The salary increases 10 to 15 percent with promotions to the lieutenant level. All firefighters and investigators within a department receive the same benefits, vacation time, sick leave, and a full retirement pension after twenty years of service.

A Look at the Job

Bob Lemons is a fire investigator for the Boca Raton, Florida, fire/rescue department. He is also the handler of Holly, an accelerant detection canine who is his partner on the job.

While Bob enjoyed his work as a firefighter, he found the investigative work more interesting. "I watched the investigators come in at a fire, and I asked a lot of questions: Why are you doing this? Why are you looking here? What are you looking for? I was persistent. After your supervisors get to know you and see that it's not just idle curiosity, they help you along."

Bob's supervisors were aware of his interest in fire investigation. Soon after he read a magazine article about accelerant canines being used by fire investigators, Bob told his chief that he would like to pursue investigation and work with a trained dog. He asked to be sent to the Maine State Police Canine Academy in Portland for five weeks, with a dog, to learn how to investigate fires.

Holly was donated by a local family and trained to search for residue of flammable liquids. Upon detection of a combustible substance, Holly signals Bob, and samples are collected and sent to a lab for examination. Holly has actually helped to catch arsonists, who sometimes linger after a fire to watch the fire department at work. Bob walks Holly through a crowd to see if she detects the scent of an accelerant on anyone nearby. The police can then arrest that person for suspected arson.

According to Bob Lemons, fire investigation is a good job that allows him to interact with many people. Bob works with local police, the state fire marshal, and federal agencies. He does say, though, that the work can be frustrating: "The rewards of this job really are few and far between. That's because you can know how a fire started, know that it was arson, but you can't prove it in a court of law. A lot of times, you learn that the insurance company had to pay the claim even though you know the owner did it. Only about 4 percent of arsonists ever get caught and convicted. You get frustrated, but inside you know you did the best job you could do. You did your part."

For More Information

International Association of Arson Investigators
12770 Boenker Road
Bridgeton, MO 63044
www.firearson.com

National Association of Fire Investigators
857 Tallevast Road
Sarasota, FL 34243
www.nafi.org

U.S. Fire Administration
16825 South Seton Avenue
Emmitsburg, MD 21727
www.usfa.fema.gov

Canadian Association of Fire Investigators
One Crimson Ridge Road
Barrie, ON L4N 8P2
Canada
www.cafi.ca

For more about Canadian firefighting, visit www.firehall.com.

Insurance Investigators

Insurance fraud is often thought of as a victimless crime, one that targets large corporations that can afford to absorb the cost of fraud. In reality, we all pay for insurance fraud since companies must raise their rates to cover their losses.

Insurance fraud is a deliberate misrepresentation of facts to an insurance carrier with the intention of defrauding the company of money. This crime can affect workers' compensation, medical, life, and property insurance. There are really no boundaries, either monetary or geographic, to insurance fraud.

Within an insurance company, investigators work in the special investigative unit and handle claims that the company suspects are fraudulent. Arson cases, false workers' disability claims, staged accidents, and unnecessary medical treatments are some of the cases that investigators might work on.

Insurance fraud investigators usually start with a database search to obtain background information on claimants and witnesses. With access to personal information such as social security numbers, driver's license numbers, addresses, criminal records, and past insurance claims, investigators can establish whether a claimant is likely to have attempted insurance fraud. Investigators might also interview claimants and witnesses, take photographs or videos, consult with lawyers, and even testify in court.

Insurance investigation often involves surveillance work, which is especially common in the case of suspected fraudulent workers' compensation claims. An investigator might carry out a long-term surveillance of a claimant to see whether he or she performs any activities that would be precluded by the stated injuries. The investigator often videotapes the claimant in any questionable activities and reports the findings to the insurance company.

Insurance fraud investigators work varied schedules due to the nature of the job. Conducting surveillance or interviewing witnesses often determine the work schedule, since claimants must be watched at different times, and witnesses are often not available during normal working hours.

The Job Requirements

While there is no specific training required for insurance fraud investigators, most insurance companies prefer to hire former law enforcement officers or private investigators for this type of work. Licensing requirements vary from state to state; check with your state's insurance department for current licensing information.

Strong interviewing and interrogation skills are important for an insurance investigator, which is one reason that former law enforcement professionals are often hired. Employers also look for candidates with ingenuity, persistence, and assertiveness.

Career Outlook and Earnings

Demand for insurance investigators should grow along with the number of claims in litigation and the number and complexity of insurance fraud cases. Competition for jobs will be strong, however, since this occupation attracts many highly qualified people, particularly those retiring from law enforcement and the military.

Salaries for insurance investigators vary widely. In 2000, the median annual earnings in the industries employing the largest number of investigators were: fire, marine, and casualty insurance, $45,060; state government, $41,620; life insurance, $39,850; insurance agents, brokers, and services, $38,960; medical service and health insurance companies, $34,560.

For More Information

For additional information about insurance investigation, including seminars and resources, visit website of the National Society of Professional Insurance Investigators at www.nspii.com.

Private Investigators

In the 1980s, TV viewers watched the exploits of Magnum, PI; readers of Sue Grafton's novels still follow the adventures of detective Kinsey Milhone. The field of private investigation can be exciting and glamorous; it can also be tedious and dull. For every undercover operation there are hundreds of hours spent on the telephone or surfing the Net, and an equal number sitting in a car at a stakeout, sipping a mug of cold coffee.

Settings for PIs

Private investigators can work for detective agencies or go it solo. They also find work either as employees or as independent contractors with insurance companies, shopping malls, hotels, and other private concerns. They can work undercover, infiltrating a ring of thieves, or sit at a desk doing background checks. They sniff out shoplifters, finger employees who are stealing, or locate missing persons. They also act as bodyguards or security guards.

Private investigators often specialize, working for a specific type of client on different cases. Legal investigators specialize in cases involving the courts and are usually employed by law firms or lawyers. Corporate investigators conduct internal and external investigations for corporations. Financial investigators may be hired to develop confidential financial profiles of individuals or companies that are prospective parties to large financial transactions (these investigators are often certified public accountants).

The Job Requirements

There are no formal requirements for most private investigator jobs, and those working in this field come from a variety of educational and business backgrounds. Many have college degrees, particularly those interested in financial investigation work.

Most private investigators have prior experience in another occupation—some have worked for insurance companies or in private security. Many former law enforcement officers and government agents become private investigators after retirement from their original jobs. Still other investigators have experience in fields such as finance, investigative reporting, and law.

Most states require private investigators to be licensed. Licensing requirements vary, but in general a convicted felon cannot be licensed, and many states are enacting mandatory training programs for private investigators. In order to carry a gun, an investigator would have to follow the appropriate state guidelines for a firearms permit.

Although there is no specified training required, employers often look for certain qualities in job applicants. Ingenuity, persistence, and assertiveness serve private investigators well. Good communication skills, the ability to think quickly, and a willingness to face confrontation are also important.

Career Outlook and Earnings

There is strong competition for private investigator positions because the field attracts many qualified people, especially those retiring from careers in law enforcement and the military. Most opportunities will be for entry-level jobs with detective agencies or as store detectives, particularly with large chains and discount stores.

Employment of private investigators is expected to be strong over the next several years, resulting from fear of crime, increased litigation, and the need to protect confidential information and property of all kinds. In addition, investigators will be needed to assist lawyers working on criminal defense and civil litigation.

Salaries for private investigators vary depending on their employer, specialty, and geographic location. Median annual earnings for private investigators in 2000 were $26,750. In department stores, which employ the largest number of investigators, median earnings were $21,180. Investigators with advanced education and work experience in positions of authority can command much higher salaries. In 2000, security/loss prevention directors and vice presidents earned a median income of $77,500.

For More Information

For additional information about becoming a private investigator, contact:

National Association of Investigative Specialists
P.O. Box 33244
Austin, TX 78764
www.pimall.com/nais

Forensic Investigators

There is no such thing as a perfect crime to forensic investigators. They are the meticulous professionals who can analyze a single hair or a drop of blood and help to catch a criminal. Forensic investigators, or forensic science technicians, collect and analyze physical evidence used in criminal investigations.

Forensic investigators often specialize in specific areas such as DNA analysis or firearm examination, performing tests on weapons or on substances such as fiber, hair, tissue, or body fluids to determine their significance to the investigation. They prepare reports based on their findings, documenting the results of the investigation and the scientific techniques used. Forensic science technicians often testify as expert witnesses in court, providing information on laboratory tests and identifying evidence.

Forensic investigation work is not for the squeamish. These investigators must collect evidence from crime scenes, and the evidence itself can be unpleasant. Body fluids, bugs, and debris of all kinds could be potentially important evidence, and all must be collected, documented, and analyzed according to specific procedures. Forensic investigators are detail oriented and curious and like to solve puzzles and mysteries.

The Job Requirements

A bachelor's degree in science is the basic requirement for a career as a forensic investigator. Courses in chemistry, biology, math, English, and computer sciences are all important, and some forensic investigators pursue graduate degrees as well. Attention to details is extremely important, as is the ability to take good notes and to write a clear scientific report. The American Academy of Forensic Sciences and the Canadian Society of Forensic Science maintain listings of several colleges and universities in the United States and Canada that offer programs in forensic science. Contact information for both organizations is listed at the end of this section.

Career Outlook and Earnings

Forensic investigation is important in all aspects of criminal cases, not only in murders. Forensic science can be used to validate a signature or resolve an issue of product liability. Investigators work in laboratories, morgues, offices, and at crime scenes. Employers include local and federal law enforcement agencies, hospitals, medical examiners, coroners' offices, and universities. Some forensic scientists work as independent consultants.

Job opportunities will be best for qualified graduates of science technician training programs. As in any competitive field, the best jobs will be available to the most highly qualified candidates.

Salaries for forensic investigators vary based on education level, job location, and type of work. In 2000, median hourly earnings of forensic science technicians were $18.04, making them the second-highest paid among science technicians after nuclear technicians.

For More Information

For information about education and careers, contact:

American Academy of Forensic Sciences
P.O. Box 669
Colorado Springs, CO 80901
www.aafs.org

Canadian Society of Forensic Science
2660 Southvale Crescent, Suite 215
Ottawa, ON K1B 4W5
Canada
www.csfs.ca

Epidemiologists

Do you follow news stories about the spread of the latest illness, wondering where it came from and where it will go next? Are you fascinated by the seemingly sudden appearance of a disease like

SARS or West Nile virus, or by cancer clusters that strike certain areas? If you would like to help solve the mysteries of how such illnesses begin, a career in epidemiology might be for you.

An epidemiologist searches for clues, collects evidence, analyzes facts, and makes connections between seemingly unrelated pieces of information. While this might sound like the work of any detective, for an epidemiologist the clues are all related to illness. The work of epidemiologists helped to identify the HIV virus, Ebola, and E. coli outbreaks.

Epidemiologists trace the frequencies and types of illnesses that occur in groups of people and the factors that influence their occurrence. Also referred to as public health, epidemiology is an increasingly important field as more virulent strains of illnesses appear throughout the world. Epidemiologists are also involved in researching the possible effects of bioterrorism.

Epidemiologists can work in a variety of settings. Every state has a Department of Public Health that employs epidemiologists. In the federal government, the Centers for Disease Control and Prevention (CDC) functions as part of the U.S. Department of Health and Human Services. Based in Atlanta, the CDC is the lead federal agency for protecting the health and safety of Americans, both at home and abroad. The National Institutes of Health (NIH) is the federal focal point for medical research in the United States. Among its twenty-seven institutes and centers, the NIH employs researchers and physicians in all fields of medicine. The main NIH campus is located in Bethesda, Maryland.

There are also private companies that employ epidemiologists. For example, a pharmaceutical company or a firm that provides services related to drug development would need to conduct epidemiological studies to better develop their products. Many epidemiologists teach in medical schools.

Epidemiology in Canada

Health Canada is the federal department charged with maintaining and improving the health of Canadians. The agency is the national center for development of health policies, enforcement of health regulations, and promotion of disease prevention. Health Canada works closely with other federal departments to reduce health and safety risks to Canadians. The national headquarters of Health Canada is located in Ottawa; regional branches are in Vancouver, Edmonton, Winnipeg, Toronto, Montreal, and Halifax.

Many major pharmaceutical companies have offices in Canada, and private organizations also employ epidemiologists for research and development projects. For those interested in teaching, several Canadian universities offer programs in epidemiology.

The Job Requirements

Anyone interested in becoming a medical detective should be skilled at collecting and analyzing data, processing information, and reasoning inductively. Most employers seeking to hire epidemiologists look for candidates with master's degrees in public health or epidemiology from accredited medical schools or universities. Many also require graduate courses in biostatistics.

In 1979 the American College of Epidemiology (ACE) was incorporated to develop criteria for professional recognition of epidemiologists and to address their professional concerns. ACE sponsors scientific meetings, publications, and educational activities. The goals of the ACE include promoting the professional development of epidemiologists through education, advocating for policies and actions that enhance the science and practice of epidemiology, and recognizing excellence in the field.

The Canadian Society for Epidemiology and Biostatistics (CSEB) was founded in 1990 for the purpose of fostering epidemiology and biostatistics research in Canada. The CSEB provides a medium for communication among professionals in the field and assists faculty or schools of medicine and public health to improve training in these disciplines. The organization brings together researchers, health care professionals, students, statisticians, and biostatisticians from across Canada and from other parts of the world.

Career Outlook and Earnings

Originally regarded as a subspecialty of medicine, epidemiology has, over the past thirty years, matured into a field of its own. In health agencies, hospitals, and research institutions, epidemiology is recognized as a distinct academic discipline and field of practice. The last several years have seen a large increase in the number of people who have entered the field of epidemiology. Many have come to the field from areas such as statistics, sociology, genetics, and biology, while others have earned graduate degrees in epidemiology or public health. The forecast for employment is strong, particularly as epidemiologists become more involved in researching the effects of bioterrorism. The continuing spread of disease throughout the world should provide ample opportunities for those interested in this field.

Salaries for epidemiologists vary widely depending on location and type of employer. In 2000, the median annual wage for epidemiologists was $48,390, with the lowest 10 percent earning $31,070 and the highest earning $78,630.

For More Information

For more information about careers in epidemiology, contact:

American College of Epidemiology
1500 Sunday Drive, Suite 102
Raleigh, NC 27606
www.acepidemiology.org

Canadian Society for Epidemiology and Biostatistics
Centre for Chronic Disease Prevention and Control
Population and Public Health Branch
Health Canada
120 Colonnade Road, PL 6702A
Ottawa, ON K1A 0K9
Canada
www.cseb.ca

Centers for Disease Control and Prevention (CDC)
1600 Clifton Road
Atlanta, GA 30333
www.cdc.gov

Health Canada
A.L. 0900C2
Ottawa, ON K1A 0K9
Canada
www.hc-sc.gc.ca

National Institutes of Health (NIH)
9000 Rockville Pike
Bethesda, MD 20892
www.nih.gov

CHAPTER SIX

Mysteries from the Past

Some mystery buffs work as diggers, both literally and figuratively—they dig for information about the past, some through mounds of dirt for relics and other evidence of past civilizations and cultures; others through mounds of paper. In this chapter, we look at a few careers that involve all sorts of digging through history.

The term *historian* covers a large range of career options and job settings. In general, historians study, assess, and interpret the past to determine what happened and why. They examine court documents, diaries, letters, and newspaper reports; they interview individuals and study archaeological and artifactual evidence. Historians conduct research, write, teach, evaluate, and make recommendations based on their findings.

Historians work in schools and universities, in libraries and museums, in government offices and private enterprises. Under the general term of *historian* come many varied career paths. This chapter examines the following job titles: archaeologist, landscape archaeologist, genealogist, archivist, art and antiquities appraiser, art authenticator, and researcher.

Archaeologists

Archaeology is a subdivision of the field of anthropology. Archaeologists study the artifacts of past cultures to learn about their history, customs, and living habits. They survey and excavate archaeological sites, recording and cataloging their finds. By careful analysis, archaeologists reconstruct earlier cultures and determine their influence on the present.

Many archaeological sites reveal details of prehistoric societies. Another area of archaeology is historical archaeology, which studies the archaeology of the modern world (A.D. 1400 to the present). The Society for Historical Archaeology defines this field as the study of the material remains of past societies that also left behind some other form of historical evidence. The main focus of the society is the era since the beginning of European exploration.

Whether prehistoric or historical, archaeological sites encompass the physical remains of past civilizations. They can include building debris and the items found inside, even trash and garbage. Usually these sites have been buried by later human activity or by natural processes. In historical archaeology, documentary evidence is also studied along with physical artifacts.

Excavation of these sites is a painstaking process conducted by professionals using modern techniques. Because these sites are so fragile, the very nature of excavating destroys some information. With this in mind, archaeologists are careful to dig only as much as they need to answer important questions. Frequently, archaeologists concentrate their work on sites scheduled to be destroyed for the construction of highways or new buildings.

Job Settings for Archaeologists

Archaeologists work in a variety of settings. Table 6.1 lists these settings and the duties specific to each.

Archaeologists conducting fieldwork often work with several other professionals in a team effort. They are assisted by geologists, ethnologists, educators, anthropologists, ecologists, and aerial photographers.

Archaeologists use a variety of tools during an excavation, including picks, shovels, trowels, wheelbarrows, sifting boxes, pressure sprayers, and brushes. Archaeologists also make drawings and sketches on site and take notes and photographs.

Table 6.1. Job Settings, Duties, and Working Conditions for Archaeologists

SETTING	DUTIES	WORKING CONDITIONS
Universities and colleges	teaching, fieldwork, research, directing student fieldwork	classrooms, labs, offices
Private institutions and museums	fieldwork, research, classifying, preserving, displaying	display and research areas, offices
Public sector (local, state, and national government agencies)	excavating, surveying, analyzing, preserving, recording	sites, labs, research facilities
Private sector (construction companies, architectural firms)	excavating, surveying, preserving, recording	sites, labs, research facilities

Do You Have What It Takes?

Do you have what it takes to become an archaeologist? Take this self-evaluation quiz to find out. Answer yes or no:

1. I have above-average academic ability.
2. I have an avid interest in science and history.
3. Hours of strenuous activity (lifting, carrying, shoveling) do not pose a problem for me.
4. I have been told I have leadership qualities.
5. The idea of continuing study throughout my career appeals to me.
6. I am a logical and analytical thinker.
7. I enjoy working independently.
8. I function well as part of a team.
9. I believe professional ethics should be strictly adhered to.
10. I can live under primitive conditions in remote areas.

To consider yourself a potential archaeologist, you must have been able to answer yes for every question. Even with just one no, you might want to reconsider your choice of career. Archaeology is an extremely rigorous and competitive profession.

The Job Requirements

To qualify as a professional archaeologist, graduate study leading to a master's degree is necessary, and a doctoral degree is often preferable. Most graduate programs in archaeology are found in anthropology departments. There are about thirty or so universities in the United States and six in Canada maintaining schools of archaeology; these are listed in *Peterson's Guide to Graduate and Professional Programs* (listed at the end of this chapter).

To gain the necessary background on the undergraduate level, pursue studies in anthropology, history, art, geology, or a related field. At the graduate level, students following a course in archaeology would also include cultural and physical anthropology and linguistics in the curriculum. The Society for Historical Archaeology lists those schools that offer programs specializing in historical archaeology.

The Archaeological Institute of America publishes the *Archaeological Fieldwork Opportunities Bulletin* (AFOB), an online resource for students and others desiring experience in archaeological excavation and survey. It includes lists of excavation opportunities, advice on preparing for participating in an excavation, and employment opportunities in field archaeology.

In addition to formal education, special preparation is required for anyone planning to be a field archaeologist. The Archaeological Institute of America posts some valuable tips on its website; some are common sense for any traveler, and others are specific to an archaeological dig. Archaeological expeditions are scientific research projects and are run by professionals working on a schedule and budget. It is important for a new member of a dig to be fully prepared and thus avoid wasting the time of the team members.

Before joining an expedition, be sure to research the local climate and culture and pack accordingly. Remember that living quarters will most likely be tight, and you will be required to carry your own belongings; therefore, it is a good idea to pack no more than you can comfortably carry on a brisk quarter-mile walk. Pack a small medical kit with some basic first-aid items, and bring along a flashlight and batteries, alarm clock, regional guidebook, and reading material.

If your expedition is in a foreign country, be sure to have all necessary documentation for travel. Depending on your destination, you might be required to have vaccinations prior to departure; it is also a good idea to have medical and dental checkups.

Career Outlook and Earnings

Job prospects for archaeologists will be better for those with advanced degrees, particularly in nonacademic settings. Competition will be strong in academia, where only the most highly qualified candidates will be offered jobs.

In 2000, archaeologists had median annual earnings of $36,040. Salaries often vary, however, according to the location and type of work.

Where the Jobs Are

Relatively few openings exist in the field of teaching archaeology. However, federal grants and contracts have made more archaeological fieldwork and research possible. A lot of this work is being conducted in western and southwestern states such as Colorado, Arizona, and New Mexico. Particularly in northwestern New Mexico there is a strong industry developing resources such as gas and oil. Much of this land is owned by the Bureau of Land Management, which employs professional archaeologists to clear the sites before gas lines or wells can be installed.

In addition, the building of a reservoir on the Dolores River in Colorado uncovered hundreds of archaeological sites, necessitating a great deal of archaeological work. The project, which is the largest on the continent and has a very generous budget, has since brought many archaeologists to that area.

Interested mystery buffs who do not desire a full-time professional career in archaeology but would like to experience archaeological work can find many opportunities to try their hands at a dig. If you are willing to invest your time, and in some cases your money, you can easily find professionally supervised archaeological investigations taking on volunteers. These are listed in *Archaeology* magazine or in the books mentioned at the end of this chapter. A few examples are provided here:

Crow Canyon Archaeological Center
23390 Road K
Cortez, CO 81321
www.crowcanyon.org

University Research Expeditions Program
UC Davis Extension
1333 Research Park Drive
Davis, CA 95616
www.urep.ucdavis.edu

Earthwatch International
3 Clock Tower Place, Suite 100
Maynard, MA 01754
www.earthwatch.org

Center for American Archeology
P.O. Box 366
Kampsville, IL 62053
www.caa-archeology.org

The Archaeological Conservancy

The Archaeological Conservancy is the only national nonprofit organization dedicated to preserving American archaeological sites. The conservancy fights to protect sites by acquiring the land and preserving it for the future. In this way, urban development, farming, and looters cannot destroy the sites and the valuable information they contain.

Since 1980 the conservancy has acquired 245 endangered sites in thirty-seven states. Ranging from a few acres to over one thousand acres, these sites span the history of North America's habitation and cultures. The conservancy owns such sites as Borax Lake in California, Singaua and Hohokam ruins in Arizona, a Seneca Iroquois village in the northeast, and ancient Indian villages in Florida. Some of the conservancy's sites have been incorporated into public parks, such as Petrified Forest National Park in Arizona, Chaco Culture National Historical Park in New Mexico, and Hopewell Culture National Historical Park in Ohio.

The Archaeological Conservancy offers tours ranging from four days to two weeks. Accompanied by expert guides, participants tour regions, such as the American Midwest, Southeast, and Southwest, as well as sites in Mexico and Central and South America. A brief sampling of tours includes Colonial Chesapeake tour, Master Potters of the Southern Deserts, Oaxaca, and California Desert Rock Art.

Crow Canyon Archaeological Center

Crow Canyon is a nonprofit research and educational institution funded by tuition fees, donations, and federal grants. The 170-acre campus in southwestern Colorado near Mesa Verde National Park promotes the preservation of the history of the Pueblo Indians of the American southwest. A staff of fifty or so archaeologists, educators, and support personnel work at Crow Canyon. In addition to their own research, they instruct participants, both adults and children, who want to learn about archaeology. From middle-school age on, participants are taken into the field and taught excavation, recording, and documentation techniques. They also work in the lab a few days a week, learning analysis techniques and methods for cleaning artifacts.

Middle school and high school students can participate in one-week programs, and an intensive three-week field school is available to older teens. Student groups from grades four through twelve can visit ongoing excavations. Adults can work on long-term research projects alongside professional archaeologists in excavation and laboratory programs. Domestic and foreign travel programs are also available.

At the time of this writing, Crow Canyon researchers are working at the Albert Porter Pueblo, a site occupied by Anasazi Indians from about A.D. 700 to the 1200s. Albert Porter Pueblo is in the heart of the Mesa Verde region of southwestern Colorado and is part of a twelve-acre archaeological preserve owned by the Archaeological Conservancy. The site is believed to have been a political and economic center for a large community.

An Archaeologist at Crow Canyon

Kristin Kuckelman is a field archaeologist at Crow Canyon Archaeological Center. Her curiosity about the field began when she was a child. Kristin's father was in the Air Force, and she traveled with her parents around the world. They were interested in different cultures and in archaeology and passed that interest on to their daughter. When she entered college, Kristin was naturally drawn to the anthropology program. She graduated with a B.A. in anthropology and psychology from Colorado Women's College (which has now merged with the University of Denver) and earned her master's degree in anthropology with a concentration in archaeology from the University of Texas at Austin.

Kristin enjoys the variety that her job offers: "I enjoy working outdoors. I enjoy writing. And with any kind of research, there's the excitement of discovery.... And basically every time you go in the field, you hope you're going to learn something about a culture that no one knew before. You don't know what that's going to be; you never really know how it's going to turn out or what you're going to find."

Kristin worked extensively on both the Sand Canyon and Castle Rock sites, which have hundreds of masonry rooms that still contain piles of rubble and thousands of artifacts. Kristen has uncovered lithic artifacts, which are made of stone, such as spear- and arrowheads, and sandstone tools for grinding grain. Tens of thousands of pottery fragments have been recovered; it is rare to find a piece that is intact.

The field season begins in early May, when Kristen and her partner prepare the areas that they plan to excavate. Paperwork and mapping are done in advance so that the team is ready for the participants to start digging.

Anyone participating in a dig at Crow Canyon first spends a full day on campus at an orientation about archaeology. Once in the field, Kristin and her partner give a site tour to outline why they are digging and what they are looking for, as well as what they hope to learn from the dig. The participants are given tools and individual instruction and work either individually or in pairs at specific locations determined by the professionals.

At the end of the season, Kristin and her partner clean and analyze the artifacts and complete their documentation and mapping. Most artifacts are put in storage, but some are placed in exhibits at the Anasazi Heritage Center, a federally run curation facility.

To maintain the integrity of the site, and for safety reasons, the areas that have been dug out during the field season are filled in with screened dirt and rocks from the site. During the winter the archaeologists write reports documenting what was learned in the summer. They also write articles for professional journals and present papers at conferences.

Archaeology in Canada

The Archaeological Survey of Canada (ASC) is the archaeology division of the Canadian Museum of Civilization. The mission of the ASC is to conduct research on the archaeology of the native peoples, or First Nations, of Canada, from the earliest occupation to the period of European settlement.

Archaeologists at the ASC undertake research, either through fieldwork or laboratory studies, which will broaden an understanding of the ancient history of Canada. At this time, current projects include Ancient Grassland Cultures in Eurasia and North America and Reconstructed Inuit Winter House, A.D. 1200–1400.

ArchaeoExpeditions is a privately run Canadian company that provides the opportunity for the public to participate in fieldwork at registered archaeological sites. For a fee, you can work with professional archaeologists on a dig. Expedition members must be eighteen years of age and receive orientation and instruction in field techniques. Participants work in small groups assigned to projects for one or two weeks.

ArchaeoExpeditions also offers opportunities for professionals. An expedition archaeologist can obtain assistance in conducting research through the company, which will assist in the recruitment of field crew, determining the necessary financial support, and marketing projects internationally.

A sampling of projects in Canada includes excavations in the Northwest Territories, Cap-de-Bon-Desir in Quebec, and the Metate Site in Ontario, where researchers explore the life of the Iroquois in Canada more than five hundred years ago. ArchaeoExpeditions also offers trips to international sites.

For More Information

For information about U.S. archaeological sites, contact:

The Archaeological Conservancy
5301 Central Avenue NE, Suite 1218
Albuquerque, NM 87108
www.americanarchaeology.com

For information about fieldwork opportunities, job placement service, and fellowships, contact:

Archaeological Institute of America
656 Beacon Street
Boston, MA 02115
www.archaeological.org

ArchaeoExpeditions
Cultural Expeditions MEC Canada, Inc.
Westgate P.O. 35012
Ottawa, ON K1Z 1A2
Canada
www.archaeoexpeditions.com

Canadian Archaeological Association
c/o Department of Anthropology and Archaeology
University of Toronto
Toronto, ON M5S 3G3
Canada
www.canadianarchaeology.com

Archaeological Society of Canada
Canadian Museum of Civilization
P.O. Box 3100, Station B
Gatineau, QC J8X 4H2
Canada
www.civilization.ca

For online listings of employment, volunteer opportunities, and useful links, visit: www.archaeologyfieldwork.com.

Landscape Archaeologists

Landscape archaeology is a field that has grown in popularity in the last decade. The purpose of landscape archaeology is to recover enough evidence to re-create a garden that existed on a specific site in a given historical period. It uses traditional archaeological techniques to recover fence lines, planting beds, and other evidence. Landscape archaeology helps determine the long-term relationship between people and their environment.

The Colonial Williamsburg Foundation in Williamsburg, Virginia, is the world's largest living history museum. Its 301-acres include hundreds of restored, reconstructed, and historically furnished buildings. But not only the buildings and costumed interpreters tell the tales of eighteenth-century colonial life. To be a true reproduction of the period, the grounds of the site must also be restored and reconstructed to their colonial appearance.

Kent Brinkley is a landscape architect in the Landscape and Facilities Services Department of the Colonial Williamsburg Foundation. He is a fellow of the American Society of Landscape Architects and past president of the Virginia Chapter. He is also coauthor, with Gordon W. Chappell, of the bestselling book, *The Gardens of Colonial Williamsburg.*

Kent describes his job as multifaceted. He works at a drawing board and creates designs for new work that is taking place. He also makes sure that gardens that were planted fifty or sixty years ago are still thriving. Many of the reconstructed gardens were designed during the 1930s and 1940s. Even though the plants chosen then are appropriate for the eighteenth century, some might not have done well in a particular setting. In these cases, Kent looks for different plants that would have been used at the time that will grow better in a particular location.

Kent works closely with the staff member who maintains the gardens. "I provide the design expertise, and we talk about what is needed in a particular garden. Once a decision has been made, he directs his maintenance staff to implement the work."

Kent is also a garden historian, which means that he has a background in history and has done research on the development of the historical landscape over time. He has traveled to England many times to visit country estates and gardens, since English landscape design served as the precedent for many of the designs in the eighteenth-century Virginia colony. Kent states, "Much of my work involves looking at what was done historically in gardens. The kinds of plants that were grown, how they were laid out, the types of fencing they were using—it's all part of knowing how to re-create a period garden."

Kent also works in conjunction with archaeologists when they excavate a site. When a particular garden site is excavated in the colonial area, Kent looks for evidence of pathways, fence lines, post holes, planting beds, and outbuilding foundations. Excavation of soil from a planting bed sometimes reveals seed materials. The soil is taken to a lab, where any particles in the soil can be extracted. Seeds are examined under a microscope to determine what type of plant they are from.

Kent has a B.A. in history from Mary Baldwin College in Staunton, Virginia. He describes his start in landscape architecture: "I'm a dying breed—you see it less and less. But I came to landscape architecture through the back door. Just as lawyers used to be able to read the law under a licensed practitioner and then sit for the bar exam, years ago you used to be able to apprentice in a landscape architecture office under a licensed practitioner. It was an equal-time commitment. In other words, when you got a five-year B.L.A. degree, you generally had to work in an office three years before you could sit for the exam. Or, in lieu of that, you could do eight years in an office and then take the exam. I waited ten years before I took the exam.

"I started as a draftsman and worked my way up to vice president of the firm before coming to Williamsburg.

"When I got my job at Williamsburg, I was ecstatic. This was the perfect marriage of my love of history and my work as a landscape architect. It's been wonderful to be able to take two major interests and combine them in a way that allows me to do both."

The Job Requirements

At this time, no American or Canadian universities offer a specific degree in landscape archaeology. Students interested in this field would have to follow a traditional program in anthropology, archaeology, or landscape architecture. Graduates with degrees in these areas could then look for jobs that would allow them to specialize and narrow their focus to landscape archaeology.

The field of landscape archaeology is still fairly small, but it is growing. Given the nature of the work, most jobs exist in living history museums such as Colonial Williamsburg, Plimoth Plantation in Massachusetts, Koontenai Brown Pioneer Village in Alberta, and Highland Village in Nova Scotia.

Genealogists

The popularity of genealogy, tracing family histories, has grown dramatically in recent years. Almost everyone has a keen interest in his or her family background.

Genealogists interview older family members; visit local courthouses, cemeteries, and libraries; and spend hours poring through diaries, old newspaper accounts, marriage licenses, and birth and death certificates.

Job Settings for Genealogists

Many genealogy hobbyists take their interest one step further and become self-employed genealogists, helping others dig up their family trees. Genealogists also are employed in historical societies and libraries with special genealogy rooms.

The Church of Jesus Christ of Latter-Day Saints in Salt Lake City, for example, maintains a huge repository of family information in its Family History Library. The library employs genealogists all over the world, including genealogists who have been accredited through its own program on a list of freelance researchers. Contact information for the Family History Library is listed at the end of this section.

Other genealogists find work teaching their skills in adult education classes, editing genealogy magazines, or writing books or newspaper columns on genealogy.

The Job Requirements

Most genealogists are not formally trained, though specializing in genealogy is possible through some university history and library science programs. Although there is not a specified curriculum for genealogists, the Board for Certification of Genealogists stresses the importance of certification for those interested in seriously pursuing this field.

Independent study courses are offered by the National Genealogical Society in Arlington, Virginia, and at Brigham Young University in Provo, Utah. The National Institute on Genealogical Research in Washington, D.C., and Samford University Institute of Genealogy and Historical Research in Birmingham, Alabama, both offer intensive five-day programs on genealogy.

In addition, many local and state genealogy societies sponsor one- and two-day seminars. Information about these seminars is published in the newsletters of both the Federation of Genealogical Societies and the National Genealogical Society. These organizations also hold annual conferences at various sites nationwide. Information about useful publications and organizations is given at the end of this section.

Earnings

According to the Society of Professional Genealogists, most genealogical practices charge by the hour and also bill for out-of-pocket expenses such as photocopies, telephone calls, travel, and vital records fees. Hourly rates range from about $15 to $100, with the average between $25 and $60. Fees vary among professionals, depending upon experience, credentials, specialty, and geographic area. Highly skilled experts who specialize in unusually difficult research problems may charge higher rates.

How to Get Started

One of the nice things about genealogy is that you can pursue it on your own before making a commitment to serious study. In this way you can decide whether this is the type of mystery solving that you enjoy.

The National Genealogical Society suggests beginning with your own family tree as an introduction to genealogy, and offers the following suggestions for how to get started.

- **Make a chart.** Begin with you, your parents, grandparents, and great-grandparents. This will be the beginning of your family tree.
- **Search for records.** Look for birth, marriage, and death certificates and any other documents that might provide names, dates, and locations. Check your family's Bible records, old letters, and photographs for clues to people's identities and relationships. Label everything you find to make it easier to organize your research.
- **Talk to family members.** Encourage older relatives to talk about their childhoods and relatives and listen carefully for clues they might inadvertently drop. Learn good interviewing techniques so you can ask questions that elicit the most productive answers. Use a tape recorder or camcorder, and try to verify each fact through a separate source.
- **Visit your local library.** Become familiar with historical and genealogical publications (a few sources are provided later in the section), and contact local historical societies. Check out the state library and the archives in your state capital. Seek out any specialty ethnic or religious libraries, and visit cemeteries.
- **Visit courthouses.** Cultivate friendships with busy court clerks. Ask to see source records, such as wills, deeds, marriage books, and birth and death certificates that are not readily available from family members.
- **Enter into correspondence.** Write to other individuals or societies involved with the same families or regions. Contact foreign embassies in Washington, D.C. Restrict yourself to asking only one question in each letter you send. Include

the information you have already uncovered. Include a self-addressed, stamped envelope and your e-mail address to encourage replies.

- **Keep painstaking records.** Use printed family group sheets or pedigree charts. Develop a well-organized filing system so you'll be able to easily find your information. Enter your research information into a database if possible. Keep separate records for each family you research.
- **Contact the National Genealogical Society.** Browse the society's online bookstore for helpful publications. You can enroll in a home-study course titled "American Genealogy: A Basic Course," or take a course through the Online Learning Center.

For More Information

The Family History Library website provides links to several useful resources, including one to locate family history centers throughout the world. For information on accreditation, contact:

Genealogical Library
Church of Jesus Christ of Latter-Day Saints
35 North West Temple Street
Salt Lake City, UT 84150
www.familysearch.org

Detailed information about the certification process, including requirements and judging procedures, is available from:

Board for Certification of Genealogists
P.O. Box 14291
Washington, DC 20044
www.bcgcertification.org

Other sources of information about training and careers in genealogy include the following:

National Genealogical Society
4527 Seventeenth Street North
Arlington, VA 22207
www.ngsgenealogy.org

Brigham Young University
Provo, UT 84602
www.byu.edu

Association of Professional Genealogists
P.O. Box 350998
Westminster, CO 80035
www.apgen.org

Federation of Genealogical Societies
P.O. Box 200940
Austin, TX 78720
www.fgs.org

Institute of Genealogy and Historical Research
Samford University
800 Lakeshore Drive
Birmingham, AL 35229
www.samford.edu

There are several guides available for the aspiring genealogist. The following volumes are recommended by the Board for Certification of Genealogists:

Board for Certification of Genealogists. *The BCG Genealogical Standards Manual.* Orem, UT: Ancestry, 2000.
Eales, Anne Bruner, and Robert M. Kvasnicka, eds. *Guide to Genealogical Research in the National Archives of the United States.* Third Edition. Washington, D.C.: National Archives and Records Administration, 2000.

Greenwood, Val D. *The Researcher's Guide to American Genealogy.* Third Edition. Baltimore: Genealogical Publishing Co., 2000.

Mills, Elizabeth Shown, ed. *Professional Genealogy: A Manual for Researchers, Writers, Editors, Lecturers, and Librarians.* Baltimore: Genealogical Publishing Co., 2001.

Archivists

Nobody knows the exact number, but it's estimated that there are close to five thousand archives in the United States. Each of the fifty states maintains a government archive, as do most city and county governments. Archives are also found in universities, historical societies, museums, libraries, and private businesses.

On the national level there is the National Archives in Washington, D.C., which looks after the records of the federal government. The Library of Congress provides information services to the U.S. Congress and technical services to all the libraries across the country.

What Are Archives?

Although archives are similar to libraries, there are distinct differences between the two. Libraries typically house materials that are published and were created with the express purpose of broad dissemination. Archives typically hold materials that were created in the course of some business or activity but were not originally intended for public use. For example, an archive might include letters from a Civil War soldier to his family. He wrote about his experiences and feelings and to let his loved ones know that he was still alive, surviving battle. He never would have imagined that his correspondence would one day appear in an archive. Inclusion in an archive gives his letters credibility and integrity as a historical source.

Archives handle collections that chart the course of daily life for individuals and businesses. Some archives specifically look after materials created by their own institutions. The Coca-Cola Company, for example, set up an archive years ago to have a history of what the company business was and how it prospered. New companies set up archives to keep documented records of their business activities.

Educational institutions such as universities or museums create archives that relate to their special research interests.

The material found in an archive can include letters, personal papers, and organizational records. Archives created within the last hundred years or so can also contain visual records, such as photographs, postcards, prints, drawings, and sketches. Today archives also collect phonograph records, audiotapes, videotapes, movie films, and computer-stored information.

Who Uses Archives?

Because archives hold firsthand information, they are valuable to anyone with an interest in the people, places, and events of the past. This group includes genealogists, museum researchers, scholars and students, writers, and historians.

What Does an Archivist Do?

As with libraries and archives, there are distinct differences between librarians and archivists, including the way they operate and the methods and techniques they use to handle material. The greatest difference is that librarians look at materials they get on an item-by-item basis. Each book is a distinct entity evaluated separately from the other books. In an archive, on the other hand, a single letter would usually be part of a larger collection of letters. Archivists are interested in these as a group because one letter would only be a fragment. To really understand something about the past, the information needs to be synthesized and put together in a collection.

When archivists talk about their work, they discuss certain basic functions that are common to all archives. The numbers following the five areas below designate the percentage of time usually spent with each duty.

Arrangement and description of collections	60%
Reference services	15%
Identification and acquisition of materials	10%
Preservation of collections	10%
Community outreach and public affairs	5%

The Job Requirements

People get into the archives profession in a variety of traditional and unusual ways. Often in a small town, an archive is a closet in the back room of a local historical society's office. Someone volunteers to put it all together, thus becoming the keeper of the community's history, or its archivist.

The standard way to become a professional archivist is to pursue a bachelor's degree in history and a graduate degree, at least at the master's level, that involves specific course work in archives. Most such graduate programs are offered through library science or history departments. Some Ph.D. programs offer archives as an option in either history or library science.

There are approximately sixty-five colleges and universities that offer courses or practical training in archival science as part of history, library science, or another discipline. At this time, there are no schools in the United States that offer a distinct master of archival studies degree. There are schools in Canada that offer the degree, which has been established according to guidelines set by the Association of Canadian Archivists.

Career Outlook and Earnings

Competition for jobs will continue to be strong as the number of qualified applicants for archivist positions increases. Graduates with extensive computer skills and specialized training, such as master's degrees in library science and history and a concentration in archives or records management, should have the best opportunities for jobs. The number of jobs is expected to grow as public and private organizations continue to establish archives and organize records and information and as public interest in science, art, history, and technology increases.

Salaries for archivists can vary greatly depending on the size and nature of the employer and often by specialty. Most government archivists have civil service status and are paid according to government wage scales. Those in academic institutions often have faculty status. In 2001, the average annual salary for archivists in the federal government, including nonsupervisory, supervisory, and managerial positions, was $63,299; archives technicians averaged $33,934. Archivists employed by large, well-funded museums can earn considerably more than those in smaller institutions. Archivists with master's degrees can expect to start out in the upper twenties to low thirties.

A Close-Up Look at the Job

John Fleckner is the chief archivist at the Smithsonian Institution's National Museum of American History. He came to the Smithsonian in 1982 with more than a decade's experience working as an archivist for the State Historical Society of Wisconsin. He is a past president of the Society of American Archivists and has acted as a consultant on many important archives projects, including the United Negro College Fund, the Vietnam History and Archives Project, and the Native American Archives Project.

John did his undergraduate work at Colgate University in Hamilton, New York, graduating in 1963 with a bachelor's degree with honors in history. He earned his master's degree in American history at the University of Wisconsin in 1965.

The archive John is responsible for acquires collections from the outside and does not handle the records generated by the museum. The collections cover a wide range of subjects and are particularly strong in the areas of American music, advertising, and the history of technology. John oversees a professional staff of twelve archivists, three student interns, and close to twenty volunteers.

John's initial interest was not in a career as an archivist. His original plan was to teach college-level history, until a university career counselor pointed him toward a graduate program in archives administration. At the time this seemed like a more profitable career choice, and John decided to pursue it.

Once John began doing archival work, he realized how much he enjoyed it. As he says, "I loved the intense, intimate contact with the 'stuff' of history. Before I completed my internship, I knew I wanted to be an archivist." During his own research as a graduate student, archived material had seemed antiseptic and lifeless to John. Once he became an archivist, though, he found the materials thrilling, and he loved "the mystery, the possibilities of the records themselves."

As an archivist, John makes decisions that will determine how future researchers access the records. In a sense, he gets to reconstruct the past and to imagine the future through the records he handles. John follows established techniques and methods and maintains standards against which his work is judged.

For More Information

Association of Canadian Archivists
P.O. Box 2596, Station D
Ottawa, ON K1P 5W6
Canada
www.archivists.ca

Society of American Archivists
527 South Wells Street, Fifth Floor
Chicago, IL 60607
www.archivists.org

Art and Antiques Appraisers

"The Antiques Roadshow" has made armchair appraisers of many of us. There's something challenging about watching the program and trying to guess the value of a particular item. If you find yourself looking at garage-sale items with a critical eye, curious about their history and wondering if they might have some hidden value, then a career in art and antiques appraisal might be for you.

The Job Requirements

Those who appraise art and antiques are called personal property appraisers; they establish a written opinion of the value of an item for a client. There are certain skills that are beneficial to anyone interested in pursuing this field.

An appraiser needs good analytical skills and the ability to work with numbers. Interpersonal skills are also very important, since appraisers usually deal directly with clients. Strong writing skills are needed to compose reports.

According to the Appraisal Foundation, a nonprofit educational organization authorized by Congress to set standards and qualifications in the field, most personal property appraisers are required to have a certain number of hours of experience in order to practice. To become a designated appraiser, you must also pass a comprehensive examination. Several appraisal organizations award designations following completion of a specific course of training done through the organization.

The Appraisal Foundation's Appraiser Qualifications Board has set voluntary minimum criteria for personal property appraisers. At present, the recommendation is for at least 1,800 hours of experience, 120 hours of education, and successful completion of a written examination. Most appraisers get their required experience hours by working as apprentices with established appraisers.

Since most appraisers receive their training through professional organizations, a college degree is not required for this career. A degree might be a requirement for advanced designations by certain organizations, but it is not a prerequisite for entering the field.

Career Outlook

The services of personal property appraisers are used by a variety of clients. Museums, insurance companies, and government agencies all need to determine the value of items they are responsible for.

As more and more people wonder about the value of those old collectables in the attic, as sales of art and antiques continue to grow, the need for personal property appraisers increases. Many private companies provide appraisal services, working for large clients or individual customers. Some even offer online appraisals, with clients scanning photos of items to be appraised. The online auction site, eBay, offers links to private companies that provide appraisals in specific areas of personal property, such as stamps, coins, paintings, and glassware.

Art Authenticators

One of the most important elements that determine the value of art and antiques is an item's authenticity. Forgery is most common in paintings, since among personal property items they are the easiest for skilled practitioners to reproduce.

Authenticating art—and, conversely, detecting forgeries—is very serious work, since so much depends on the decision of the professional. Many serious collectors spend thousands of dollars on a single painting, and even the average consumer who decides to invest a small sum in art does not want to be swindled.

Museums and galleries must be able to authenticate items they plan to acquire. In these settings, authentication may be part of the work done by a curator, gallery owner, or professional art authenticator.

The Job Requirements

Authenticating art requires very good technical skills. While there are some basic visual signs that indicate a painting's authenticity, a thorough examination includes the use of forensic techniques, computer diagnostic models, and spectral and chemical analysis. A solid background in art history and familiarity with painting techniques are also needed, as are strong computer skills.

Museum specialists, art dealers, and gallery owners are usually very knowledgeable about the visual methods of validating a painting. They often specialize in a particular artist, genre, or period and are familiar with, or have access to, the catalogues raisonnés of many famous artists. A catalogue raisonné is a book containing photographs of the works of a deceased artist, as well as other important identifying information about each work.

One of the aspects of authentication that is fun for a mystery buff is determining the provenance of a painting. The provenance is the history of the painting's ownership and can add greatly to an item's value. A painting that has been widely exhibited at different museums will often be valued more highly than a work of similar quality that has not been exhibited. Even the history of the frame can add value to a painting.

To determine provenance, you must be prepared to search for any records that pertain to the painting in question. Sales receipts, documents of ownership, and gallery or museum records are some of the clues that can help you to solve your puzzle.

Sometimes it is the history of an item's ownership that becomes important to collectors. In 1990, Sotheby's New York auctioned items belonging to the late actress Greta Garbo. A painting by the French artist Albert Andre sold for $170,000, four times more than any of his work had ever commanded at auction. In 1994, Sotheby's auctioned another of Andre's paintings, which brought only $23,000. It seems apparent that the earlier painting sold for so much money because of its history as part of Greta Garbo's collection.

A Close-Up Look at the Job

Matthew Carone is the owner of Carone Gallery in Fort Lauderdale, Florida. He handles mainly contemporary art: American, some European, and some Latin American paintings and sculpture. His discovery of a forged Picasso helped establish his career.

Matthew dealt in original prints, many of which came from Europe. Despite being color blind, he is able to detect the lightness or darkness of a color quite clearly. It was this ability that led him to detect a discrepancy in the shade of black used in a Picasso print, which he could tell was different from the original work.

The print was ultimately shown to Picasso, who returned it with the word *faux,* or fake, written across it. Picasso signed the print, which ended up giving some value to the forgery. The FBI became involved in the case but was not able to determine the identity of the forger. As a result of his detective work, Matthew Carone was asked to look at other Picasso works and developed a reputation for his ability to determine authenticity.

For More Information

American Society of Appraisers
555 Herndon Parkway, Suite 125
Herndon, VA 20170
www.appraisers.org

The Appraisal Foundation
1029 Vermont Avenue NW, Suite 900
Washington, DC 20005
www.appraisalfoundation.org

Canada Personal Property Appraisers Group
1881 Scanlan Street
London, ON N5W 6C3
Canada
www.cppag.com

Researchers in Living History Museums

Researchers can find work in a variety of conventional settings: university archaeology and history departments, preservation boards, libraries and archives, and government offices. Carolyn Travers works in an unconventional place: a living history museum. She serves as the director of research at Plimoth Plantation in Plymouth, Massachusetts.

Researchers are the backbone of every living history museum. Without their efforts, the accurate re-creation of authentic period characters, restoration of historic buildings, or reproduction of a facsimile of daily life would be an impossible task.

Plimoth Plantation consists of four sites: the 1627 Pilgrim Village, the Mayflower II, Hobbamock's Wampanohg Indian Homesite, and the Carriage House Crafts Center. Every aspect of each program must be researched to present as authentic a picture as possible of seventeenth-century life. Carolyn might research anything, as she says, "from what was the period attitude toward toads, how a character felt about being her husband's third wife, or the correct way to cook a particular dish to some obscure point of Calvinist theology."

Research generally includes the life and genealogical background of a character. According to Carolyn, it is more difficult to research the female characters because there is less documented information available about them than about the males. The researchers use several sources, including court records and genealogical research done by professionals from such organizations as the General Society of Mayflower Descendants or writers for genealogy periodicals.

Other types of research are handled by different departments. For example, re-creating authentic buildings and structures is the responsibility of the curatorial department.

Carolyn Travers attended Earlham College, a small Quaker school in Richmond, Indiana, where she earned a bachelor's degree in fine arts with a concentration in history. She went on to

Simmons Graduate School of Library and Information Science in Boston and graduated in 1981 with master's degree in library and information science with a concentration in research methods.

The Job Requirements

Carolyn Travers points out that researching is a competitive field and that a higher degree, specifically in history or library science with a research methods concentration, is necessary.

A candidate is not expected to have a general body of knowledge about the specific time period, but he or she must have strong research skills, talent, and experience.

Earnings

New graduates might begin with a salary in the low twenties. As Carolyn Travers stresses, "You don't do it for the money. There are a lot of psychological payments. One of the satisfactions for me is to be able to change someone's mind about the stereotypes surrounding early colonists."

For More Information

Peterson's Guide to Graduate Schools and Professional Programs
www.petersons.com
Visit the website for a searchable database of graduate schools in the United States and Canada. The site provides complete information on schools and programs, as well as guides to admissions essays, test preparation, financial aid, and resume services.

The following magazines are important resources for living history researchers:

Archaeology (www.archaeology.org)
National Geographic (www.nationalgeographic.com/ngm)
Scientific American (www.scientificamerican.com)
Smithsonian (www.smithsonianmag.si.edu)

The following professional journals, though not available in every local library, can be found in university libraries or in large public libraries. All provide abstracts of articles free of charge online, unless otherwise noted.

American Antiquity (www.saa.org/publications/index.html)
Historical Archaeology (www.sha.org/sha_ha.htm)
Journal of Anthropological Archaeology
   (www.elsevier.com/locate/issn/0278-4165)
Journal of Field Archaeology (http://jfa-www.bu.edu/)
North American Archaeologist (www.baywood.com)

CHAPTER SEVEN

Mysteries of Science

A mystery buff could get lost in this vast area of career possibilities that use research and investigative skills. The field of science covers everything from the human mind to animal behavior, from medical research to the far-off planets in the universe. It would take an encyclopedia to cover all the choices. So in true detective style, the best suggestion is for you to use this chapter as a starting-off point. Once you've narrowed the field, you'll have to continue your research, digging up more information on the various careers. Some resources have been listed for you at the end of this chapter and in the appendix.

Mysteries of the Mind

Many mystery buffs are intrigued by the human mind. What makes us tick? How do we learn? What motivates us? What causes us to react, think, and feel the way we do?

Psychologists

As a mystery buff you might have read Jonathan Kellerman's books featuring the hero Alex Delaware. He's a child psychologist who inevitably gets involved playing the role of detective as well as doctor for his troubled patients.

Most psychologists don't get involved in police matters (unless they are working for or with the police). But they do conduct a special kind of detective work, probing the human psyche, trying to understand the human condition in order to offer help to individuals and groups.

Psychologists study human behavior and mental processes to understand, explain, and change people's behavior. They may study the way a person thinks, feels, or behaves. Research psychologists investigate the physical, cognitive, emotional, and social aspects of human behavior. Psychologists in applied fields counsel and conduct training programs; do market research; apply psychological treatments in a variety of medical and surgical situations; and provide mental health services in hospitals, clinics, and private settings.

Like other social scientists, psychologists formulate hypotheses and collect data to test their validity. Research methods depend on the topic under study. Psychologists may gather information through controlled laboratory experiments; personality, performance, aptitude, or intelligence tests; observation, interviews, or questionnaires; clinical studies; or surveys. Computers are widely used to record and analyze this information.

The knowledge gained by psychologists is used in a variety of settings, including health and human services, management, education, law, and sports. In addition to the variety of work settings, psychologists usually specialize in one of many different areas.

Clinical Psychologists. Clinical psychologists constitute the largest specialty, generally working in independent or group practices or in hospitals or clinics. They may help the mentally or emotionally disturbed adjust to life, and they are increasingly helping medical and surgical patients deal with their illnesses or injuries. They may work in physical medicine and rehabilitation settings, treating patients with spinal cord injuries, chronic pain or illness, stroke, arthritis, or neurological conditions such as multiple sclerosis. Others help people deal with life stresses such as divorce or aging.

Clinical psychologists interview patients; give diagnostic tests; provide individual, family, and group psychotherapy; and design and implement behavior-modification programs. They may collaborate with physicians and other specialists in developing treatment programs and helping patients understand and comply with the prescribed treatment.

Some clinical psychologists work in universities and medical schools, where they train graduate students in the delivery of mental health and behavioral medicine services. Others administer community mental health programs. Counseling psychologists use several techniques, including interviewing and testing, to advise people on how to deal with problems of everyday living, whether personal, social, educational, or vocational.

Developmental Psychologists. These professionals study the patterns and causes of behavioral change as people progress through life from infancy to adulthood. Some concern themselves with behavior during infancy, childhood, and adolescence, while others study changes that take place during maturity and old age. They also study developmental disabilities and their effects.

Educational Psychologists. Elementary and secondary schools or school district offices employ psychologists to resolve students' learning and behavior problems. Also called school psychologists, they collaborate with teachers, parents, and school personnel to improve classroom management strategies or parenting skills, counter substance abuse, and work with students with disabilities as well as gifted and talented students. They also evaluate the effectiveness of academic programs, behavior management procedures, and other services provided in the school setting.

Experimental Psychologists. These research-oriented psychologists study behavior processes and work with human beings and with animals such as rats, monkeys, and pigeons. Also called research psychologists, they work in university and private research centers and in business, nonprofit, and governmental organizations.

Prominent areas of experimental research include motivation, thinking, attention, learning and retention, effects of substance use and abuse, sensory and perceptual processes, and genetic and neurological factors in behavior.

Industrial-Organizational Psychologists. By applying psychological techniques to personnel administration, management, and marketing problems, these psychologists seek to improve productivity and the quality of the working environment. They are involved in policy planning, applicant screening, training and development, psychological test research, counseling, and organizational development and analysis. They often work as consultants, brought in by management to solve a particular problem.

Social Psychologists. Social psychologists examine people's interactions with others and with the social environment. Prominent areas of study include group behavior, leadership, attitudes, and interpersonal perception. They typically work in organizational consultation, marketing research, systems design, or other applied psychology fields.

Subspecialties in Clinical Psychology. The field of clinical psychology includes four subspecialties that are rapidly gaining in popularity:

- **Cognitive psychologists** deal with the brain's role in memory, thinking, and perceptions. Some cognitive psychologists do research related to computer programming and artificial intelligence.
- **Health psychologists** promote good health through health maintenance counseling programs. Programs might be designed, for example, to help people stop smoking or lose weight.
- **Neuropsychologists** study the relation between the brain and behavior. They often work in stroke and head-injury programs.

- **Geropsychologists** deal with the special problems faced by the elderly.

The emergence and growth of these specialties reflects the increasing participation of psychologists in providing direct services to special patient populations. Other areas of specialization include psychometrics; psychology and the arts; the history of psychology; psychopharmacology; and community, comparative, consumer, engineering, environmental, family, forensic, population, military, and rehabilitation psychology.

Sociologists

Those in the know postulate that while psychologists really enter the field to understand and change themselves, sociologists want to be able to take on and change the world around them. Sociologists study human society and social behavior by examining the groups and social institutions that people form: families, communities, and governments, as well as various social, religious, political, and business organizations. They also study the behavior and interaction of groups, trace their origin and growth, and analyze the influence of group activities on individual members. They are concerned with the characteristics of social groups, organizations, and institutions; the ways individuals are affected by each other and by the groups to which they belong; and the impact of social traits such as gender, age, and race on a person's daily life.

As a rule sociologists work in one or more specialties, such as social organization and mobility; racial and ethnic relations; education; family; social psychology; urban, rural, political, and comparative sociology; or gender roles and relations. Other specialties include medical sociology, the study of social factors that affect mental and public health; gerontology, the study of aging and the special problems of the elderly; environmental sociology, the study of the effects of the physical environment and technology on people; clinical sociology, therapy, analysis, and intervention for individuals, groups, organizations, and communities; demography, the study of the size, characteristics, and movement of populations; criminology, the study of factors producing deviance from accepted legal and cultural norms; and industrial sociology, the study of work and organizations. Some sociologists specialize in research design and data analysis.

Sociologists usually conduct surveys or engage in direct observation to gather data. For example, after providing for controlled conditions, an organizational sociologist might test the effects of different styles of leadership on individuals in a small work group. A medical sociologist might study the effects of terminal illness on family interaction. Sociological researchers also evaluate the efficacy of different kinds of social programs. They might examine and evaluate particular programs of income assistance, job training, health care, or remedial education.

Sociologists extensively use statistical and computer techniques in their research, along with qualitative methods such as focus-group research and social impact assessment.

The results of sociological research aid educators, lawmakers, administrators, and others interested in resolving social problems and formulating public policy. For example, sociologists study a wide range of issues related to abortion rights, AIDS, high school dropouts, homelessness, and latchkey children. Sociologists often work closely with community groups and members of other professions, including psychologists, physicians, economists, statisticians, anthropologists, social workers, urban and regional planners, political scientists, and law enforcement and criminal justice officials.

Sociologists often are confused with social workers, and in fact both kinds of professionals do contribute to one another's disciplines. Whereas most sociologists conduct research on organizations, groups, and individuals, clinical sociologists—like social workers—may directly help people who are unable to cope with their circumstances.

Training for Psychologists and Sociologists

A doctoral degree generally is required for employment as a psychologist. Psychologists with a Ph.D. qualify for a wide range of teaching, research, clinical, and counseling positions in universities, elementary and secondary schools, private industry, and government. Psychologists with Psy.D. (doctor of psychology) degrees qualify mainly for clinical positions. An educational specialist (Ed.S.) degree qualifies a person to work as a school psychologist.

A master's degree in psychology allows a person to administer tests as a psychological assistant. Under the supervision of a doctoral-level psychologist, the assistant can conduct research in laboratories, conduct psychological evaluations, counsel patients, and perform administrative duties. In addition, with a master's degree one can teach in high schools or two-year colleges or work as a school counselor.

A bachelor's degree in psychology qualifies a person to assist psychologists and other professionals in community mental health centers, vocational rehabilitation offices, and correctional programs; to work as a research or administrative assistant; and to take a job as a trainee in government or business. However, without additional academic training, advancement opportunities in psychology are severely limited.

A master's degree in sociology usually is the minimum requirement for employment in applied research or community college teaching. The Ph.D. degree is essential for most senior-level positions in research institutes, consulting firms, corporations, and government agencies and is required for appointment to permanent teaching and research positions in colleges and universities.

Sociologists holding master's degrees can qualify for administrative and research positions in public agencies and private businesses. Training in research, statistics, and computer methods is an advantage in obtaining such positions.

Bachelor's degree holders in sociology often get jobs in related fields. Their training in research, statistics, and human behavior qualifies them for entry-level positions in social services, management, sales, personnel, and marketing. Many work in social service agencies as counselors or child care, juvenile, or recreation workers. Others are employed as interviewers or as administrative or research assistants. Sociology majors with sufficient training in statistical and survey methods may qualify for positions as junior analysts or statisticians in business or research firms or government agencies. Regardless of a sociologist's level of education, completion of an internship while in school can prove invaluable in finding a position in sociology or a related field.

Career Outlook and Earnings

Employment for psychologists is expected to grow fastest in the health care areas of outpatient mental health and substance-abuse treatment clinics. Many job opportunities will also arise in schools, public and private social service agencies, and management consulting services.

Private companies employ psychologists in survey design, analysis, and research to provide marketing evaluation and statistical analysis. An increase in employee assistance programs, which offer employees help with personal problems, should also spur job growth.

Graduates with master's degrees in school psychology should have the best job prospects, as schools are expected to increase student counseling and mental health services. Master's degree holders with several years of business and industry experience are qualified for jobs in consulting and marketing research.

For sociologists, job prospects will be best for those with advanced degrees. Government agencies, social service organizations, marketing departments, research and consulting firms, and a wide range of businesses employ sociologists. Competition for academic jobs will be strong, but many jobs are available for sociologists in nonacademic settings.

Salaries for both psychologists and sociologists vary greatly according to the degree held, the area of specialization, and the geographic area in which the psychologist or sociologist works. The median annual earnings of salaried psychologists in 2000 were $48,596; for clinical, counseling, and school psychologists, $48,320; and for industrial-organizational psychologists, $66,880. The federal government recognizes education and experience in certifying applicants for entry-level positions. In general, the starting salary for psychologists with a bachelor's degree was about $21,900 in 2001; those with superior academic records began at $27,200. Psychologists with master's degrees and one year of experience could start at $33,300. Psychologists with Ph.D. or Psy.D. degrees and one year of internship could start at $40,200, and some with greater experience start at $48,200. The average annual salary for psychologists in the federal government was $72,830.

Sociologists had median annual earnings of $45,670 in 2000. In the federal government, starting salaries for bachelor's degree holders with no experience were $21,900 or $27,200, depending on college records. Those with master's degrees could start at $33,300, with doctorates at $40,200. Some applicants with experience and advanced degrees started at $48,200.

Experienced sociologists with doctoral degrees tend to earn the highest salaries in academia. Those employed in business, industry, and private consulting may earn more than those in academia or in government. The master's degree may be as lucrative as a doctorate in some settings outside of academia.

In general, sociologists with Ph.D. degrees earn substantially higher salaries than those with lesser degrees. Some sociologists supplement their salaries with earnings from other sources, such as consulting, counseling, or writing articles and books. Those who create their own consulting practices find that earnings vary according to how much time they devote to their practice, the type of clients they serve, and the region of the country.

For More Information

For information on education, accreditation, and licensing in psychology and sociology, contact:

American Psychological Association
750 First Street NE
Washington, DC 20002
www.apa.org

Canadian Psychological Association
151 rue Slater Street, Suite 205
Ottawa, ON K1P 5H3
Canada
www.cpa.ca

For information on education, research, funding, and careers, contact:

American Sociological Association
1307 New York Avenue NW, Suite 700
Washington, DC 20005
www.asanet.org

Information on careers and certification in the United States and Canada is available from:

Association of State and Provincial Psychology Boards
P.O. Box 241245
Montgomery, AL 36124
www.asppb.org

For information about clinical and applied sociology, visit the Sociological Practice Association website at www.socpractice.org.

Mysteries of the Universe

If you are content to leave the mysteries of the mind and society to others and are more intrigued by the universe and its vast number of questions, then you might be a mystery buff who would like to solve some of the puzzles the universe has to offer.

Career Options

There are almost as many job possibilities as there are puzzles. All sorts of scientists study all sorts of mysteries of the earth—on land, underwater, or in space. The questions presented here suggest a range of occupations involved in searching for the answers.

On Land. How was our planet formed? Can we predict earthquakes? How can we find oil and other natural resources? How can we best grow crops? How can we save our endangered animals? How can we protect our environment? How can we better plan our cities and roads?

- Geologists
- Engineers
- Environmentalists
- Agricultural scientists
- Ecologists
- Zoologists
- Urban planners
- Developers

Underwater. How were the oceans formed? What natural resources lie below the oceans? What kind of marine life exists in the seas?

- Geologists
- Oceanographers
- Marine biologists

In Space. What are the conditions on other planets and moons? How can we travel more efficiently to distant planets? How can space exploration help us on Earth?

- Engineers
- Astronauts
- Astronomers
- Educators

On Land: Geologists

Mystery buffs who are interested in the history of the earth might appreciate a career in geology. Geologists study the composition, processes, and history of the earth. They try to find out how rocks were formed and what has happened to them since formation. They also study the evolution of life by analyzing plant and animal fossils. Geologists are part of a larger group, called geoscientists, who study the earth's geologic past in order to make predictions about its future.

Geologists often spend much of their time in the field, identifying and examining rocks, studying information collected by remote-sensing instruments in satellites, conducting geological surveys, constructing field maps, and using instruments to measure the earth's gravity and magnetic field. For example, they often perform seismic studies, which involve bouncing energy waves off buried rock layers, to search for oil and gas or to understand the structure of rock layers below the earth's surface.

Working in laboratories, geologists examine the chemical and physical properties of specimens. They study fossil remains of animal and plant life or experiment with the flow of water and oil through rocks. Geologists use a variety of sophisticated laboratory and computer instruments.

Subspecialties of Geology. There are numerous subspecialties that fall under the major discipline of geology. Here is a brief look at a few of these titles.

- **Petroleum geologists** explore for oil and gas deposits by studying and mapping the subsurface of the ocean or land.

They use sophisticated geophysical instruments, well log data obtained from exploration and recovery digging, and computers to interpret geological information.

- **Engineering geologists** apply geologic principles to the fields of civil and environmental engineering, offering advice on major construction projects and assisting in environmental remediation and natural hazard reduction.
- **Mineralogists** analyze and classify minerals and precious stones according to composition and structure and study their environment in order to find new mineral sources.
- **Paleontologists** study fossils found in geologic formations to trace the evolution of plant and animal life and the geologic history of the earth.
- **Stratigraphers** study the formation and layering of rocks to understand the environment in which they were formed.
- **Vulcanologists** investigate volcanoes and volcanic phenomena to try to predict the potential for future eruptions and possible hazards to human health and welfare.

The Job Requirements. A bachelor's degree in geology is acceptable for some entry-level jobs. However, better jobs with good advancement potential usually require at least a master's degree in geology. A master's degree is required for most entry-level research positions in colleges and universities, federal agencies, and state geological surveys. A doctorate is necessary for most high-level research positions.

Hundreds of colleges and universities in the United States offer bachelor's degrees in geology. In Canada, more than two dozen universities offer programs in geoscience. The majority of programs include classical geologic methods and topics (mineralogy, petrology, paleontology, stratigraphy, and structural geology). Students studying physics, chemistry, biology, mathematics, engineering, or computer science may also qualify for some geoscience positions if their course work includes study in geology.

Students interested in working in the environmental or regulatory fields, either in environmental consulting firms or federal and state governments, should take courses in hydrology, hazardous waste management, environmental legislation, chemistry, fluid mechanics, and geologic logging.

Geologists usually work as part of a team with other scientists, engineers, and technicians. For this reason, excellent interpersonal skills are a must. Strong writing skills are also useful because of the number of technical reports and research proposals that must be written.

Some geologists work in offices, but many others split their time between fieldwork and an office or laboratory. An increasing number of exploration geologists work in foreign countries, often in remote areas and under difficult conditions. Geologists often travel to remote field sites by helicopter or four-wheel drive vehicle and cover large areas on foot. They should be physically fit and have the stamina necessary to work comfortably in the field.

Career Outlook and Earnings. In the past, employment of geologists has been cyclical and largely affected by the price of oil and gas. When prices were low, oil and gas producers curtailed exploration activities and laid off geologists. When prices were high, companies had the funds and incentive to renew exploration efforts and hire geologists in large numbers.

In recent years, a growing worldwide demand for oil and gas and new exploration and recovery techniques, particularly in previously inaccessible sites, have returned some stability to the petroleum industry, with some companies increasing their hiring of geologists.

Opportunities are expected to increase for geologists in foreign countries as construction and exploration for oil and natural gas continues abroad. The need for companies to comply with environmental laws and regulations should contribute to the demand for engineering geologists. An expected increase in highway building and other infrastructure projects will also be an additional source of jobs for engineering geologists.

Median annual earnings of geoscientists were $56,230 in 2000. The middle 50 percent earned between $43,320 and $77,180. The lowest 10 percent earned less than $33,901, and the highest 10 percent earned more than $106,040.

For More Information

For information on careers in the geosciences, contact:

Geological Association of Canada
Department of Earth Sciences
Room ER4063, Alexander Murray Building
Memorial University of Newfoundland
St. John's, NF A1B 3X5
Canada
www.gac.ca

Geological Society of America
P.O. Box 9140
Boulder, CO 80301
www.geosociety.org

Underwater: Oceanographers

Oceanography, like geology, is one of the geosciences. Oceanographers use their knowledge of geology and geophysics, in addition to biology and chemistry, to study the world's oceans and coastal waters. They study the motion and circulation of the ocean waters and their physical and chemical properties and how these properties affect coastal areas, climate, and weather. Oceanographers are often linked professionally with scientists who study limnology, which is the scientific study of bodies of fresh water for their biological, physical, and geological properties. Oceanography also has several subcategories:

- **Physical oceanographers** study the ocean tides, waves, currents, temperatures, density, and salinity. They study the interaction of various forms of energy, such as light, radar, sound, heat, and wind with the sea, in addition to investigating the relationship between the sea, weather, and climate. The work of physical oceanographers provides the maritime fleet with up-to-date oceanic conditions.
- **Chemical oceanographers** study the distribution of chemical compounds and chemical interactions that occur in the ocean and sea floor. They may also investigate how pollution affects the chemistry of the ocean.
- **Geological and geophysical oceanographers** study the topographic features and the physical makeup of the ocean floor. Their knowledge can help oil and gas producers find these minerals on the bottom of the ocean.
- **Biological oceanographers** study the distribution and migration patterns of the many diverse forms of sea life in the ocean. Biological oceanographers are also called marine biologists.

The required education and training for oceanographers is basically the same as for geologists. The most highly qualified candidates, with the best educational records, will get the best jobs. There are about thirty-five colleges and universities in the United States that offer master's degree programs in oceanography. In Canada, six universities offer master's level oceanography degrees.

For More Information

To learn more about careers exploring underwater mysteries, visit the website or contact:

American Society of Limnology and Oceanography
5400 Bosque Boulevard, Suite 680
Waco, TX 76710
www.aslo.org

In Space: Astronomers

Any mystery buff who is interested in exploring the heavens, who wonders about the mysteries of the universe and would love to uncover some of its secrets, might be well suited to a career in astronomy. Astronomers use the principles of physics and mathematics to learn about the fundamental nature of the universe, including the sun, moon, planets, stars, and galaxies. They also apply their knowledge to solving problems in navigation, space flight, and satellite communications and to developing the instrumentation and techniques used to observe and collect astronomical data.

Almost all astronomers do research. Some are theoreticians, working on the laws governing the structure and evolution of astronomical objects. Others analyze large quantities of data gathered by observatories and satellites and write scientific papers or report on their findings.

Some astronomers actually operate, usually as part of a team, large space- or ground-based telescopes. However, astronomers may spend only a few weeks each year making observations with optical telescopes, radio telescopes, and other instruments, then use the rest of their time to analyze the information gathered.

For many years, satellites and other space-based instruments have provided tremendous amounts of astronomical data. New technology resulting in improvements in analytical techniques and instruments, such as computers and optical telescopes and mounts, is leading to a resurgence in ground-based research.

A small number of astronomers work in museums housing planetariums. These astronomers develop and revise programs presented to the public and may direct planetarium operations.

The Job Requirements. Most jobs are in basic research and development, so a doctoral degree is the usual educational requirement for astronomers. For those seeking permanent positions in basic research in universities or in government laboratories, additional experience and training in a postdoctoral research appointment is also important. Many doctorate-level astronomers teach in colleges and universities.

About sixty-nine universities in the United States offer degrees in astronomy, either through astronomy, physics, or combined physics/astronomy departments. Competition is strong for places in astronomy doctoral programs. In Canada, nine schools offer astronomy or physics/astronomy programs. Students planning a career in astronomy should have a very strong physics background; an undergraduate degree in either physics or astronomy is excellent preparation.

Mathematical ability, problem-solving and analytical skills, an inquisitive mind, imagination, and initiative are important traits for anyone planning a career in astronomy. Good oral and written communication skills are also valued because of the need to write research papers or proposals.

Career Outlook and Earnings. Generally, many astronomers have been employed on research projects, often defense related. Defense expenditures are expected to increase in coming years, so employment of astronomers is projected to grow. The federal government funds several noncommercial research facilities with physics-related research departments, as well as other agencies such as NASA. If funding continues to grow at these agencies, job opportunities for astronomers, especially those dependent on federal research grants, should be better than they have been in many years.

Graduates with only bachelor's degrees in astronomy are not qualified to enter most research positions but may qualify for a wide range of positions in engineering, technician, mathematics, and computer- and environment-related occupations. Those who meet state certification requirements can become high school teachers. Those with a strong physics background will find their skills useful in many occupations.

The median annual earnings of astronomers in 2000 were $74,510.

For More Information

American Astronomical Society
2000 Florida Avenue NW, Suite 400
Washington, DC 20009
www.aas.org

Canadian Astronomical Society
Department of Physics
Queens University
Kingston, ON K7L 3N6
Canada
www.casca.ca

National Space Society
600 Pennsylvania Avenue SE, Suite 201
Washington, DC 20003
www.nss.org

A Close-Up Look at Planetariums

Most of us have visited a planetarium at some time and can recall the thrill of sitting in a darkened dome, watching the night sky move above and around us. With an impressive voice explaining the spectacle, we witnessed solar and lunar eclipses, the solar corona, comets, auroras, and other astronomical phenomena.

For many of us, this is all that we remember of our school field trip to the planetarium. For some, however, that visit was the first of many. If you wonder how the special effects are achieved and how you might be part of this interesting world, read on to learn more about how planetariums work.

The Hayden Planetarium, New York. In February 2000, the renovated Hayden Planetarium opened in New York City. The largest and most powerful virtual-reality simulator in the world, the Hayden Planetarium is part of the new Rose Center for Earth and Space at the American Museum of Natural History.

At the heart of the planetarium is the Space Theater, where "Passport to the Universe," a three-dimensional space ride, is presented. A one-of-a-kind projector and digital system are used to fly audiences through the galaxy and beyond. By simulating flight through the largest data-based model of the universe ever projected, the viewer is virtually taken to the surface of any object in the solar system.

The Hayden Planetarium's show is based on actual astronomical data and computer models of our galaxy obtained from the National Aeronautics and Space Administration (NASA), including the Hubble Space Telescope. Other sources include a statistical database of more than three billion stars developed by the museum. For sections of the galaxy for which there is no available data, the museum constructed statistical models that were translated into high-definition computer simulations of the galaxy.

The projector used in the Hayden Planetarium is completely computer controlled and can project more than nine thousand stars onto the dome, along with the sun and planets. Thirty times each second, the supercomputer calculates the real location and appearance of every star and nebula that is about to be seen by the audience. Fiber optics generates a starry sky that includes objects normally viewable only through binoculars.

Scientists, imagery analysts, programmers, graphic designers, and educators are building a visual database of the two hundred thousand observed stars, pulsars, and nebulae that have been charted in astronomical catalogs. The computer system can generate statistically correct stars to represent the two hundred million uncharted stars in the galaxy, up to five billion stars for any one presentation.

A smaller exhibit is the Big Bang, which contains a central thirty-six-foot screen over an eight-foot-deep bowl around which visitors gather, standing on plexiglass flooring. The show uses lasers, dozens of lighting effects, an LED display, narration, and surround sound to immerse viewers in the imagery and energy of the early universe.

The Hayden Planetarium also houses other exhibit halls that present such phenomena as cosmic evolution; the formation of galaxies, stars, and planets; the collision of galaxies; and the formation of a supernova.

It clearly takes many people with varied skills to put together something as detailed as a planetarium show. Here is a list of some of the jobs to be done:

- **Producers** bring together all the elements of a show. Media experience is important in this capacity.
- **Technicians** construct, maintain, and install stationary exhibits and may make sound tracks or special-effects devices. A bachelor's degree or degree from a technical or trade school, and related experience, is usually required.
- **Artists** create images for use in some shows. Computer graphics, airbrushing, and other media are used in many instances.
- **Astronomers** translate research into information accessible to the general public. Planetariums that are affiliated with universities or have an observatory employ staff astronomers who teach and conduct research. A doctorate is usually required; a master's degree is acceptable in some cases.
- **Educational Programmers/Coordinators** develop ideas for shows and research materials for them. A background in astronomy is a plus, and a master's degree is required for most jobs in this area.
- **Scriptwriters** use information and research to write the narrative parts of shows. A scriptwriter might be on staff at a planetarium or could work as a freelancer.
- **Presenters** handle the live portion of a show and interact with the audience, which often consists of schoolchildren. Good communication skills are a plus.

Career Outlook and Earnings. There are many planetariums throughout the United States and Canada, ranging from those as large as New York's Hayden Planetarium or Toronto's Ontario Science Centre to small institutions maintained by local school districts. In any setting, it takes a number of people to keep a planetarium running. As our interest in science and space travel grows, the number of visitors to planetariums increases each year.

One good way to secure a position in a planetarium is to volunteer. Many planetariums announce job openings to other planetariums, and being present as a volunteer or intern can give you an edge to learning about new positions.

The size and location of the planetarium dictates most earnings. An experienced producer at a larger institution might earn between $40,000 and $50,000; a producer in a small regional planetarium would earn considerably less.

Salaries vary from institution to institution, but even in large cities, salaries are not glamorous. A recent job posting for an assistant curator at a small planetarium, requiring a bachelor's degree and one year of experience, lists an annual salary in the low twenties. Astronomers with doctoral degrees will earn high salaries, since they are often tenured faculty members at affiliated universities. The amount of experience and education you bring to the position and your location will determine how much you earn.

A Close-Up Look at a Professional

Noreen Grice is operations coordinator at the Charles Hayden Planetarium at Boston's Museum of Science. She has a bachelor's degree in astronomy from Boston University and a master's in astronomy from San Diego State University.

Noreen describes her position as less a researcher and more an educator and liaison between the research and the public. Her background in astronomy qualifies her to translate the research into information that can be presented to the public and to check the scientific accuracy of the scripts for the planetarium's shows.

Noreen's job has included coordinating special events such as Astronomy Day and Space Week. Astronomy Day is an international event intended to spark interest in astronomy. She contacts astronomy clubs and local small planetariums to invite them to set up display tables. There are special shows to be arranged, and Noreen invites speakers to give talks on different topics.

Noreen Grice also teaches courses at the planetarium. When she began working at the Hayden Planetarium, the only classes offered were very specialized classes for adults. She created courses for children ranging from preschool through high school. The classes cover the earth and moon, sun and stars, and the planets. Today she is one of several instructors for many courses offered.

Part of Noreen's job includes answering questions from the public and letters from schoolchildren. She initially wrote individual replies to each letter, but when it became apparent that specific questions were asked repeatedly, Noreen composed fifteen brochures on different astronomy topics.

Noreen's advice to anyone hoping to work in a position similar to hers is to study astronomy. In her opinion, "It would give you an edge over the competition and peace of mind knowing in your heart that what you're reading is accurate." Astronomy will also give you the foundation to interpret the research being done.

For More Information

Job listings in planetariums are available through:

International Planetarium Society
P.O. Box 1812
Greenville, NC 27835
www.ips-planetarium.org

CHAPTER EIGHT

Mysteries off the Beaten Path

Mystery buffs who are unafraid to work outside the norm, are not put off by being doubted, and are comfortable as the center of attention might find careers in some slightly unconventional areas. In this chapter, we look at three somewhat off-beat career paths: paranormal investigators, coordinators of mystery walking tours, and mystery theater groups.

Unsolved Mysteries

Do you believe in ghosts and spirits and haunted houses? What about extrasensory perception and psychokinesis? UFOs? The Loch Ness Monster? Crop circles?

Did you see *Signs* or *The Sixth Sense*? Do you watch "Crossing Over" or "Sightings"? Do books by Anne Rice and Stephen King keep you up all night, turning pages?

Maybe, or maybe not. When it comes to the realm of the paranormal, there are the believers, those who cannot be shaken from their stand, and the nonbelievers, those who will never be convinced. Some people fall in between: the show-me group of people who keep an open mind but would need hard evidence to move them off the fence.

The strong beliefs of some, either for or against, have led to some interesting careers. But be forewarned—job opportunities in this area are few and far between. Only a small fraction of dedicated believers or debunkers have been able to carve a niche for themselves in this controversial territory.

What Does It All Mean?

Every discipline has its own jargon. Before we forge ahead, it's a good idea to have a few definitions in our arsenal.

- **Paranormal** describes activity outside or beyond the reach of present-day scientific thought or knowledge.
- **Psychic phenomena,** when considered in relation to the human mind, usually fall into two categories: extrasensory perception (ESP) and psychokinesis (PK).
- **ESP** is the ability to obtain information without the benefit of the senses. It is usually split into two subcategories: telepathy, the ability to perceive someone else's thoughts, and clairvoyance, the ability to sense an object or event outside the range of the senses.
- **Psychokinesis,** or PK, is the ability of the mind to influence animate or inanimate matter without the use of any known physical or sensory means. In other words, it is the ability to move or alter matter by thought alone. PK includes: telekinesis, the ability to move objects; levitation, the ability to overcome gravity and rise or float in the air; materialization, the ability to cause a spirit or other nonphysical being to take a bodily form; and paranormal healing, the ability to cure disease or affliction by no known scientific means. It also refers to poltergeist activity, mysterious events such as rappings, overturned furniture, and flying objects.
- **Parapsychology** is the study of psychic phenomena.
- **Spiritualism** is a system of beliefs focused on efforts to communicate with the dead or with spirits. Channelers facilitate communications between earthly and spirit worlds. Some channelers also attempt contact with extraterrestrials or spirits from ancient mythical societies, as well as with the

recently deceased. Channelers are also sometimes referred to as mediums. Automatic writing is a way for spirits to communicate with the living. A medium or channeler holds a pen and pad of paper, then enters a trance. This allows the spirit to express his or her thoughts using the medium's hand.

A Little History

Interest in psychic phenomena can be traced back to early times. The first modern organizations to investigate such phenomena were the British Society for Psychical Research, founded in 1881, and the American Society for Psychical Research, founded in 1885.

Much of the early investigation conducted by these two groups was unscientific and anecdotal in nature. J. B. Rhine, a psychologist at Duke University in Durham, North Carolina, wanted to change the approach and methods used. He began his work investigating parapsychology in 1927. In the course of his work, Rhine coined the term *extrasensory perception*. In 1935, Duke eventually allowed him to split from the psychology department and form the first parapsychological laboratory in the country. Over twenty years ago, the parapsychology department and Duke University parted ways, but those carrying on Rhine's work did not want to let it die. They soon formed the Institute for Parapsychology, which is also located in Durham, North Carolina.

The Controversy. The majority of scientists outside the field of parapsychology do not accept the existence of psychic phenomena. As a result, they do not accept the discipline of parapsychology. In scientific thinking, in order to study something, there has to be something there to study.

The most weighty criticism launched against parapsychologists is that of fraud. Rhine himself discovered that one of his researchers had been faking results, and the man was dismissed.

Parapsychologists counter this charge by saying that they do well in policing their own ranks.

Another charge is that parapsychologists are not trained to tell whether a subject is committing fraud. Even amateur magicians have been known to fool investigators. Parapsychologists insist that this type of fraud happens only in an insignificant number of cases.

Another major criticism is that for ESP, PK, and other phenomena to be true, basic physical laws would have to be broken. To counter that, some parapsychologists believe that breakthroughs in particle physics may one day provide explanations for such phenomena. Others feel that paranormal activity operates outside the realm of science. Toward the end of his life, the great psychologist Carl Jung suggested that the deepest layers of the unconscious function independently of the laws of space, time, and causality, allowing for paranormal phenomena.

Other charges against parapsychology include shoddy experimental design, incorrect statistical interpretations, and misread data. A study in 1988 conducted by the National Research Council maintained that no scientific research in the past 130 years had proven the existence of parapsychological phenomena. The council did, however, find anomalies in some experiments that could not readily be explained. Parapsychologists claim that the study was biased because the members of the research committee were nonbelievers.

A Close-Up Look at a Paranormal Investigator

Joe Nickell is one of the few paid paranormal investigators in the country. He's a staff member of the Committee for the Scientific Investigation of Claims of the Paranormal (CSICOP), which is based at the Center for Inquiry, a nonprofit international organization with headquarters in Amherst, New York.

Joe has had an interesting and colorful career. He has worked as a private investigator, a professional stage magician at the Houdini

Hall of Fame (under the stage names Janus the Magician and Mendell the Mentalist), a blackjack dealer, a riverboat manager, a newspaper stringer, a historical and literary investigator, and a writer of articles and books (see a listing at the end of the chapter). He has also managed to find time to earn bachelor's, master's, and doctoral degrees, all in English literature, from the University of Kentucky at Lexington.

While working at the Houdini Hall of Fame, Joe met James Randi (the Amazing Randi), who was involved in paranormal investigation. Joe thought that exposing psychics as Randi did was interesting and exciting. He soon had the opportunity to investigate a haunted house called Mackenzie House, a historic building in Toronto where various phenomena were occurring late at night. Caretakers heard footsteps on stairs when no one was there, among other unexplained sounds.

Joe discovered that the sounds were all illusions: "They were real sounds, but they were coming from the building next door. The buildings were only forty inches apart, and the other building had a staircase made of iron that ran parallel to the Mackenzie House stairway. Whenever anybody went up and down the stairs next door, it sounded as if it was coming from within the Mackenzie House. The interesting thing to me was that no one had figured this out for ten years."

A mystery buff who is also a skeptic might, like Joe Nickell, want to see proof of paranormal claims. In Joe's case, his skepticism led him to conduct his own investigations. He was in the Yukon Territory working as a blackjack dealer and writing an occasional newspaper piece when he met a group of men claiming that they could use their dowsing wands to find gold. Joe challenged the men to prove their claim under controlled test conditions, and they agreed. He put gold nuggets in some boxes padded with cotton. Other boxes contained fool's gold or nuts and bolts, and some were left empty. The boxes were all put into a sack; even Joe didn't know which contained the real gold. Psychic ability would have been the only way any of the men could have known what was in each box, and as Joe says, "of course they failed the test miserably." He ended up writing an article about the experiment.

Whenever Joe heard of an interesting claim, he investigated it himself. He worked on a major investigation of the Shroud of Turin, disproving the claim that the image on the shroud could not be duplicated. Joe proved that the image could indeed be duplicated using a simple process, and his results were published in several magazines.

Joe's work on the Shroud of Turin was noticed by the Committee for Scientific Investigation of Claims of the Paranormal. Founded by such distinguished names as Paul Kurtz, Carl Sagan, and Isaac Asimov, CSICOP was established to investigate claims of the paranormal. The founders were responding to the sensationalism of paranormal claims on television and in tabloids and wanted to form a society that could address the issue. In Joe's words, "CSICOP was set up to investigate—not to dismiss out of hand, not to start out to debunk, but simply to investigate—claims of the paranormal. And if that meant debunking, so be it."

Joe volunteered for years for CSICOP and was hired full-time in 1995. "The center needed a detective, a magician, a writer, and a researcher, and by hiring me they got all of them in one." He describes himself as "a magic detective." While parapsychologists believe there is some power of the mind to read people's thoughts or divine the future, they know that there is no scientific evidence for any of this. Investigation has revealed many claims to be false, often due to tricksters using sleight of hand. This is Joe's area of expertise.

Joe has been a guest on several television shows, including "Larry King Live," "Sally Jessy Raphael," "Maury Povich," and "Charles Grodin." He describes his appearances as "the token skeptic. They put on the believers, the UFO abductees and so forth, and I get a minute at the end to say, 'Bah humbug.'" He has also been a consultant on "Unsolved Mysteries" many times. He resolved a case of some photographs taken in Kentucky that supposedly showed the image of the Virgin Mary. His investigation proved that the miraculous image was in fact caused by sunlight and the superimposition of a protector card onto the film when the photos were taken.

Unlike some less scrupulous investigators, Joe and his colleagues use real methods to investigate claims, not tricks. They interview people, search for evidence, and look for causes. They do not use machinery or gadgets, since there is no scientific evidence that such methods prove or disprove the paranormal.

Joe is most interested in the investigative aspect of his work and finds solving mysteries the most rewarding part of his job. He has even challenged himself by looking back through history for the solutions to long-ago puzzles, which sounds like fascinating work for a mystery buff.

For example, there is a story about Oliver Lerch, an Indiana boy who disappeared in the 1890s after being sent to draw water from the family well. His tracks ended halfway to the well, and he was gone. The story has been published many times, always as an unsolved mystery.

Joe began to investigate, and found through a deed search that no family named Lerch ever owned property in the area. Some stories claimed that the incident was still in the police files, but a search revealed that the police had no record of it. Joe proved that Oliver Lerch never disappeared, because Oliver Lerch never even existed. In fact, Joe found that the story is more or less a plagiarized version of an old Ambrose Bierce horror tale called "Charles Ashmore's Trail."

Advice from a Professional. Joe Nickell has some advice for mystery buffs interested in a career investigating the paranormal:

- Read the literature, particularly the skeptical literature. The believers will mislead you with phony stories like the Oliver Lerch tale. The CSICOP journal, *The Skeptical Inquirer,* is a good starting point. The journal publishes reviews of books and articles on the paranormal.

- Learn something about magic. It's helpful in understanding how people can be fooled and what the different tricks are.
- Depending on the area you're most interested in, journalism, psychology, and astronomy are useful. Psychology would be good for investigating people who feel they're possessed or haunted or have been abducted by aliens.
- Develop your people skills. Investigators rely on each other and share information; collaboration is often essential.
- To pursue a career, investigate phenomena and turn your material into articles. A writer specializing in this area could make some money. Joe cautions, however, that "if you are really interested in being a freelance writer and making a buck, you need to be on the other side of the belief coin. You can sell a pro-ghost story far easier than you can sell one that debunks it. But if truth and honesty matter to you, you will not sell out. You will report fairly and thoroughly."

For More Information

There are few university programs in this country now devoted to training parapsychologists or their counterpart debunkers. Undergraduate-level courses and a thirty-hour certificate of proficiency are available from:

Center for Inquiry
P.O. Box 741
Amherst, NY 14226
www.centerforinquiry.net

Links to education and training sources can be found through:

Centre for Parapsychological Studies in Canada
Box 29091, 7001 Mumford Road
Halifax, NS B3L 4T8
Canada
www.cpscghosts.com

Rhine Research Center
2741 Campus Walk Avenue, Building 500
Durham, NC 27705
www.rhine.org

General information about parapsychology is available from:

American Society for Psychical Research
5 West Seventy-Third Street
New York, NY 10023
www.aspr.com

Committee for the Scientific Investigation of Claims of the
    Paranormal (CSICOP)
CSICOP
Box 703
Amherst, NY 14226
www.csicop.org

You can also use your finely tuned sleuthing skills to track down
training programs from the resources listed below.

Hines, Terence. *Pseudoscience and the Paranormal.* Amherst, NY:
    Prometheus Books, 2001.
LeShan, Lawrence. *The Medium, the Mystic, and the Physicist:
    Toward a General Theory of the Paranormal.* New York:
    Allworth Press, 2003.
Center for Inquiry. *The Skeptical Inquirer.* P.O. Box 703, Amherst,
    NY 14226.

You may also be interested in the following books, written by
Joe Nickell:

Real-Life X-Files: Investigating the Paranormal. University of
    Kentucky Press, 2001.

Inquest on the Shroud of Turin: Latest Scientific Findings.
Prometheus Books, 1999.

Looking for a Miracle: Weeping Icons, Relics, Stigmata, Visions and Healing Cures. Prometheus Books, 1999.

Pen, Ink, and Evidence: A Study of Writing and Writing Materials for the Penman, Collector, and Document Detective. New Castle, Delaware, 2002.

Mystery for Fun and Profit

Many innovative people have combined their love of a good mystery with other talents or acquired skills. A dedicated mystery buff can use a good imagination to bring in extra income or create a specialized career. Here is one successful venture that might spark some ideas of your own.

Mystery Walking Tours

If you're comfortable talking with small groups of people, like to walk, know how to conduct research, and can put together a one-to two-hour presentation, then starting a mystery walking tour might be a fun way to bring in some additional earnings.

Basically, the leader of a mystery walking tour escorts a group of (paying) people to designated sites and landmarks in a particular area. At each stop, the leader gives a talk on that specific spot, telling about its history or notoriety and answering questions.

Mystery walking tours are usually organized around a particular theme. Stops on the route can cover homes of famous mystery writers or focus on where crimes or scandals occurred. For example, a tour of Boston could follow the killing spree route of the Boston Strangler. The popularity of *Midnight in the Garden of Good and Evil* has spawned several tours in Savannah, Georgia. New Orleans is ripe with legend, mystery, and intrigue, and even an island as small as Key West has had its share of titillating incidents. Some tours focus on the paranormal, others on actual documented events.

How far you can go with this idea depends in part on where you live and how active criminals or mystery writers are in your area. Follow these ten steps to get started:

1. Research your area. Visit the public library, check out courthouse records, or ask to be allowed into the newspaper morgue. Search the Internet for past events or notorious residents, but remember they must all be within walking distance of each other.

2. If your research is fruitful, decide how long a tour you can develop with the material you have. Then organize your information to follow the different stops you'll make. Allow ten minutes or so for each spot. Get as many juicy details as possible. Gory and gruesome details work well, too. (Remember, everyone loves a good mystery!)

3. Decide on a price. A ninety-minute to two-hour walking tour costs on average $20 per person. You can give discounts for children or senior citizens. The more you have in your group, the more you'll make.

4. How often will you offer the tour? Every Saturday morning? Sunday afternoons? Some of the scarier tours are offered at night, when darkness adds to the sense of mystery. If the area warrants it, you could run one or two a day. It's up to you.

5. Make a dry run. Walk the tour with friends and family and practice your presentation. It's unlikely that you'll be able to enter any of the buildings without making some sort of arrangement with owners, so be sure to pick out a spot where you and your group can pause to talk. Under a shady tree is good for summer days, but be careful not to block vehicular or pedestrian traffic.

6. Check with local officials regarding any zoning restrictions or occupational licenses or permits you might need.

7. Prepare your pamphlets. You'll need to design and print a brochure that details your tour, how people can contact

you, the times and dates you operate, and how much the
tour costs. Be sure to mention if any part of your tour
includes steep or uneven terrain that participants should
know about in advance; you don't want anyone falling
behind or unable to complete the tour. And though it
might seem obvious, mention that customers should wear
comfortable walking shoes.

8. You're now ready to make the leap into tour leader. You'll
   want to stop in at various hotels, visitor centers, chambers
   of commerce, historical societies, and any other spots
   frequented by tourists or residents to ask if you can leave
   promotional pamphlets on display for prospective customers. Your plan will most likely be met with enthusiasm.
   Establishments that cater to tourists are usually glad to
   help advertise events. Many hotels already keep racks in
   their lobbies filled with pamphlets for various local
   attractions.

9. Find additional ways to promote your tour. Create a press
   release to send to newspapers; most local papers regularly
   publish a calendar of events. Contact local radio stations
   and cable television stations, and drop in at bookstores
   (a favorite hangout for mystery buffs). Make arrangements
   for your tour to be included on Internet sites about your
   city's attractions.

10. Invest in a pair of good walking shoes, dig out the sun-
    screen, and get ready to have fun. (Panama hat is optional.)

A Close-Up Look at a Walking Tour Guide

In Chapter 2, we met mystery writer David Kaufelt. While orga-
nizing the first Key West Literary Seminar, David put together
a mystery walking tour of the island to entertain the seminar
participants.

David describes Key West as the scene of many mysteries and
murders that have never been solved. He had done some research

on them for an article he wrote, and that led to the idea to start the mystery walking tour, which became a good way to raise money for the Key West Literary Seminar.

David did some research on the different houses and some of the events he knew of that had happened in his lifetime. For example, a young man and an older man shared a mansion around the corner from David's former home. The two fought quite often, and no one had seen the younger man for quite some time. It came to light that the younger man was an alcoholic and had died, but the older man didn't acknowledge his death.

As David describes it, "He thought he was just being ornery. So he'd go get him food every day and told people how he would never speak to him, he was so ornery. But then we all started smelling something strange, and the police were finally notified. The young guy had been dead for months and had almost melted into the linoleum floor in the kitchen. The older man's mind had gone, and his family came and took him away and put him someplace."

David's tours also include the cemetery, where there is always an interesting murder story to talk about.

Some Advice for Tour Guides. David Kaufelt offers some advice for anyone interested in starting a mystery walking tour:

- Do your research very well and be entertaining. You need to be able to tell an anecdote with a punch line.
- Try to get an organization behind you, such as Mystery Writers of America or Sisters in Crime. You might also become associated with an Elderhostel program in your area. People come to a city to learn, and such organizations can put together different events for them.
- Make sure you have something with which to identify yourself for people who will be meeting you on a street corner. It could be a T-shirt with a logo printed on it or a banner you can wave.

For More Information

The following books provide insight into the business of mystery walking tours.

Dale, Alzina. *Mystery Reader's Walking Guide: New York*. Lincoln, NE: iUniverse, Inc., 2002.

Dale, Alzina, and Barbara Sloan Hendershott. *Mystery Reader's Walking Guide: Chicago*. Lincoln, NE: iUniverse, Inc. 2002.

....

Put Murder on the Menu

The last several years has seen the rise of a form of entertainment especially designed to appeal to mystery buffs. No longer do restaurant goers have only their companions and food to keep them occupied. Some enterprising entrepreneurs have arranged for a waiter or waitress, a cook, or perhaps even someone dining at your table to keel over dead in front of your eyes. Shot, stabbed, or maybe even poisoned.

Whodunit? That's for diners to figure out. Here are two professional companies that produce mystery theater dinner shows.

Grace Bentley Theatrical Productions

Adriana and Rick Rogers own Grace Bentley Theatrical Productions, based in Carmel, New York. They formed the company in 1999 to produce mystery theater shows. According to Adriana, their original intention was to rent scripts from an established distributor, but she and Rick found the scripts to be below their standards. They had a particular level of entertainment in mind, and the scripts they were seeing didn't meet their criteria. Adriana says that too many were "low brow, not family-oriented. I would have been embarrassed to put my name on the shows."

Adriana and Rick wanted to present family-oriented shows that they could feel comfortable performing for school groups as well as adults. After realizing that there weren't any available scripts that they wanted to use, they decided to write their own material. They had written a play before and knew that they could write material that they would be proud to perform before any audience. As Adriana says, "plays are like your children, and you don't trust your children to just anyone."

They started with a show set in the 1940s, *The Zoot Suit Swing Time Murders.* The show centers around a band performing in a dance hall; one of the members is murdered. There are lots of clues to help the audience figure out who the killer is, and plenty of incentive as well. Audience members get to participate in the action, as the cast interacts with diners, dropping hints and clues, trying to throw the dining detectives off the track. Once the murder is solved, prizes are given to those who correctly guess the identity of the killer.

Based on the success of this show, Rick and Adriana wrote two more scripts. *Murder at the Sock Hop* is set in the 1950s, and *Death at the Disco* is set in the 1970s. They employ about fifteen actors, including understudies. Most of their actors work in more than one show. Adriana acts in all three shows, and Rick serves as an understudy. His main job during performances is to run the sound board, so he prefers not to act since it means he will have to do two jobs at once. Rick would rather devote his time to the sound system to be sure that it is run correctly for each show. Adriana and Rick do all the backstage work themselves.

When Grace Bentley first began, Adriana placed ads in newspapers to attract customers. Now, however, all of their advertising is either by word of mouth or run by the establishments where they perform. For instance, audience members often approach Adriana and Rick after a show to ask if they will perform at a fundraiser or similar event. The organization sponsoring the event prepares the advertising. When they are scheduled to do a show at a restaurant, the restaurant handles the advertising.

Adriana and Rick perform in a variety of settings. They do public shows at restaurants as well as fundraising events and private parties. They were even hired to perform their *Zoot Suit Swing Time Murders* show at a wedding reception.

The establishments at which they perform also set the ticket price for a performance. Adriana used to handle ticket sales but is now happy to let the establishments take care of it. Tickets usually range from $35 to $50, depending on the type of event.

For a private event, the fee is $1,375, or $25 per person, whichever is the higher amount. There is a discounted price for senior citizens. Restaurants also receive a discount to offset the cost of their advertising the event.

All of the actors have full-time professional careers outside of acting, so they do this work for the love of it. The actors are paid a set fee, plus any tips, and their meals are always included. Adriana offers a "loyalty incentive," increasing an actor's pay after twelve performances. She is always willing to let any interested actors audition for the company.

Adriana and Rick don't do this work full-time but for their own enjoyment. Rick is a respiratory therapist, and Adriana is a secretary and planning to attend school for stenography. They perform about one show every six weeks or so, and Adriana handles their bookings.

Getting Started. Aside from imagination and energy, there are a few things you need to start your own mystery theater business. If you want to put on professional-quality shows, Adriana advises that you invest in a sound system. The system used by Grace Bentley Productions cost about $10,000, but Adriana considers it money well spent. Their actors all wear body mikes, which are important when you are performing in a large room. Without the microphones, audience members at the back of the room miss important clues and bits of information in the show.

In addition, you need costumes—Adriana and Rick now need costumes for three different shows, since they are all set in different decades. Sets, music, advertising, and office space and equipment are all factors in establishing your business. And don't forget that, if you won't be writing your own scripts, you will need to pay royalties.

Some Advice for Mystery Theater Types. Adriana Rogers has a few tips for anyone interested in working in mystery theater.

- Adriana loves her work, but she cautions that it has to be taken seriously: "It's really fun, but it's still work. You still have to maintain your professional attitude even if your character is kooky."
- As a performer, you must be very mindful of your audience. Many people prefer to watch the show quietly and don't want to participate; some love to be involved in the action. Experience will tell you which people don't want to be pulled into the story; don't force them up onto the dance floor. There are always plenty of people who want to jump right in and have a good time.
- Invest in the best sound system you can afford because it will only enhance the audience's appreciation of the show and add to the quality of your performances.

MurderWatch Mystery Theater

Another company that combines love of mystery with the drama of theater is MurderWatch Mystery Theater. Connie and Jeffrey Gay produce, direct, and write a series of shows that they perform in Orlando, Florida.

After several years of performing in musical theater, Connie and Jeffrey wanted to try something new. They saw that mystery shows were becoming popular and decided to write their own material, add music, and get the audience involved in the action. They have been performing weekly at the Grosvenor Resort Hotel for more than ten years: "Every Saturday night, guests get to play detective, and they also might become suspects. We make sure that there's activity in every section of the room. We make it so everyone sees something, no one sees everything, and everyone gets caught in the act." They have recently also begun performing at the Garden Eatery in St. Augustine.

The Finances Involved. When MurderWatch Mystery Theater began, Connie and Jeffrey realized it would be difficult to manage if they only took a cut of the sales, since attendance varied. As Connie says, "Some nights we'd get 150 people; some, only 80. But we still had to pay the same expenses. We agreed to charge a flat fee. The fee can vary from hotel to hotel. We pay the actors and buy our own equipment. We also have our own liability insurance." A ticket at the Grosvenor Hotel costs $39.95; at the Garden Eatery, $24.95

The actors, musicians, and technicians are all independent contractors. The company uses about thirty-five different actors, musicians, and technicians. There are six different shows, each using eight to ten performers.

Pay Attention to the Business in Show Business. Connie says that an advantage that she and Jeffrey have is their theater background and awareness of the business aspect of what they do: "Jeff worked for eight years in a bank and . . . I worked eight years as a computer analyst. You can't organize yourself and a group of people, especially people with egos, if you don't have a solid business background.

"In the theater everyone becomes close and like family, and it's fun to be able to keep that atmosphere like we do, but it is a business, and you can't lose sight of that fact. If you do, and you get lax, you can fail.

"We have our long-term goals, and we know where we're heading as a business. And the fun we have along the way is the fringe benefits. There's always a let's-put-on-a-show atmosphere, but we never lose sight of the bottom line.

Professional Associations

T he following list of associations can be used as a valuable resource guide in locating additional information about specific careers. Many of the organizations provide information about education and internship opportunities, and some post job listings. Most of the associations' websites include links to even more helpful sites and resources.

American Academy of Forensic Sciences
P.O. Box 669
Colorado Springs, CO 80901
www.aafs.org

American Anthropological Association
2200 Wilson Boulevard, Suite 600
Arlington, VA 22201
www.aaanet.org

American Astronomical Society
2000 Florida Avenue NW, Suite 400
Washington, DC 20009
www.aas.org

American Bar Association
541 North Fairbanks Court
Chicago, IL 60611
www.abanet.org

American College of Epidemiology
1500 Sunday Drive, Suite 102
Raleigh, NC 27607
www.acepidemiology.org

American Historical Association
400 A Street SE
Washington, DC 20003
www.theaha.org

American Library Association
50 East Huron
Chicago, IL 60611
www.ala.org

American Psychological Association
750 First Street NE
Washington, DC 20002
www.apa.org

American Society of Appraisers
555 Herndon Parkway, Suite 125
Herndon, VA 20170
www.appraisers.org

American Society of Journalists and Authors
1501 Broadway, Suite 302
New York, NY 10036
www.asja.org

American Society of Limnology and Oceanography
5400 Bosque Road, Suite 680
Waco, TX 76710
www.aslo.org

American Society for Psychical Research
5 West Seventy-Third Street
New York, NY 10023
www.aspr.com

American Sociological Association
1307 New York Avenue NW, Suite 700
Washington, DC 20005
www.asanet.org

The Appraisal Foundation
1029 Vermont Avenue NW, Suite 900
Washington, DC 20005
www.appraisalfoundation.org

The Archaeological Conservancy
5301 Central Avenue NE, Suite 1218
Albuquerque, NM 87108
www.americanarchaeology.com

Archaeological Institute of America
656 Beacon Street
Boston, MA 02215
www.archaeological.org

Archaeological Society of Canada
Canadian Museum of Civilization
100 Laurier Street
P.O. Box 3100, Station B
Gatineau, QC J8X 4H2
Canada
www.civilization.ca

Association of Authors' Representatives, Inc.
P.O. Box 237202, Ansonia Station
New York, NY 10003
www.aar-online.org

Association of Canadian Archivists
P.O. Box 2596, Station D
Ottawa, ON K1P 5W6
Canada
www.archivists.ca

Association of Professional Genealogists
P.O. Box 350998
Westminster, CO 80035
www.apgen.org

Association of State and Provincial Psychology Boards
P.O. Box 241245
Montgomery, AL 36124
www.asppb.org

Canadian Archaeological Association
c/o Department of Anthropology and Archaeology
University of Toronto
Toronto, ON M5S 3G3
Canada
www.canadianarchaeology.com

Canadian Association of Fire Investigators
One Crimson Ridge Road
Barrie, ON L4N 8P2
Canada
www.cafi.ca

Canadian Association of Journalists
Algonquin College
1385 Woodroffe Avenue, B224
Ottawa, ON K2G 1V8
Canada
www.eagle.ca/caj

Canadian Astronomical Society
Department of Physics
Queens University
Kingston, ON K7L 3N6
Canada
www.casca.ca

Canadian Bar Association
500-865 Carling Avenue
Ottawa, ON K1S 5S8
Canada
www.cba.org

Canadian Journalism Foundation
117 Peter Street, Third Floor
Toronto, ON, M5V 2G9
Canada

Canada Personal Property Appraisers Group
1881 Scanlan Street
London, ON N5W 6C3
Canada
www.cppag.com

Canadian Psychological Association
151 rue Slater Street, Suite 205
Ottawa, ON K1P 5H3
Canada
www.cpa.ca

Canadian Society for Epidemiology and Biostatistics
Centre for Chronic Disease Prevention and Control
Population and Public Health Branch
Health Canada
120 Colonnade Road, PL 6702A
Ottawa, ON K1A 0K9
Canada
www.cseb.ca

Canadian Society of Forensic Science
2660 Southvale Crescent, Suite 215
Ottawa, ON K1B 4W5
Canada
www.csfs.ca

Centre for Parapsychological Studies in Canada
Box 29091, 7001 Mumford Road
Halifax, NS B3L 4T8
Canada
www.cpscghosts.com

Committee for the Scientific Investigation of Claims of the
    Paranormal (CSICOP)
Center for Inquiry
P.O. Box 703
Amherst, NY 14226
www.csicop.org

Crime Writers of Canada
3007 Kingston Road, Box 113
Toronto, ON M1M 1P1
Canada
www.crimewriterscanada.com

The Dow Jones Newspaper Fund
P.O. Box 300
Princeton, NJ 08543
http://djnewspaperfund.dowjones.com

Federation of Genealogical Societies
P.O. Box 200940
Austin, TX 78720
www.fgs.org

Genealogical Library
Church of Jesus Christ of Latter-Day Saints
Family History Library
35 North West Temple Street
Salt Lake City, UT 84150
www.familysearch.org

Geological Association of Canada
Department of Earth Sciences
Room ER4063, Alexander Murray Building
Memorial University of Newfoundland
St. John's, NF A1B 3X5
Canada
www.gac.ca

Geological Society of America
P.O. Box 9140
Boulder, CO 80301
www.geosociety.org

Institute for Parapsychology
Rhine Research Center
2741 Campus Walk Avenue, Building 500
Durham, NC 27705
www.rhine.org

Institute of Genealogy and Historical Research
Samford University
800 Lakeshore Drive
Birmingham, AL 35229
www.samford.edu/schools/ighr

International Association of Arson Investigators
12770 Boenker Road
Bridgeton, MO 63044
www.firearson.com

International Planetarium Society
P.O. Box 1812
Greenville, NC 27835
www.ips-planetarium.org

International Union of Police Associations
1421 Prince Street, Suite 400
Alexandria, VA 22314
www.iupa.org

Mystery Writers of America, Inc.
17 East Forty-Seventh Street, Sixth Floor
New York, NY 10017
www.mysterywriters.org

National Association of Broadcasters
1771 N Street NW
Washington, DC 20036
www.nab.org

National Association of Fire Investigators
857 Tallevast Road
Sarasota, FL 34243
www.nafi.org

National Association of Government Archives and Records
   Administrators
48 Howard Street
Albany, NY 12207
www.nagara.org

National Association of Investigative Specialists
P.O. Box 33244
Austin, TX 78764
www.pimall.com/nais

National Fire Protection Association
Batterymarch Park
Quincy, MA 02269
www.nfpa.org

National Genealogical Society
4527 Seventeenth Street North
Arlington, VA 22207
www.ngsgenealogy.org

National Library and Archives of Canada
395 Wellington Street
Ottawa, ON K1A 0N3
Canada
www.archives.ca

National Newspaper Association
P.O. Box 7540
Columbia, MO 65205
www.nna.org

National Society of Professional Insurance Investigators
NSPII National
P.O. Box 88
Delaware, OH 43015
www.nspii.com

National Space Society
600 Pennsylvania Avenue SE, Suite 201
Washington, DC 20003
www.nss.org

Newspaper Association of America
1921 Gallows Road, Suite 600
Vienna, VA 22182
www.naa.org

Organization of American Historians
112 North Bryan Avenue
Bloomington, IN 47408
www.oah.org

Radio-Television News Directors Association
RTNDA
1600 K Street NW, Suite 700
Washington, DC 20006
www.rtnda.org

Sisters in Crime
P.O. Box 442124
Lawrence, KS 66044
www.sistersincrime.org

Society for American Archaeology
900 Second Street NW, Suite 12
Washington, DC 20002
www.saa.org

Society of American Archivists
527 South Wells Street, Fifth Floor
Chicago, IL 60607
www.archivists.org

Society for Historical Archaeology
19 Mantua Road
Mt. Royal, NJ 08061
www.sha.org

Sociological Practice Association
Department of Sociology and Anthropology
St. Cloud State University
St. Cloud, MN 56301
www.socpractice.org

Statistics Canada (Census Bureau)
Statistical Reference Centre
R.H. Coates Building, Lobby
Holland Avenue
Ottawa, ON K1A 0T6
Canada
www.statcan.ca

U.S. Census Bureau
4700 Silver Hill Road
Washington, DC 20233
www.census.gov

U.S. Fire Administration
16825 South Seton Avenue
Emmitsburg, MD 21727
www.usfa.fema.gov

U.S. National Archives and Records Administration
8601 Adelphi Road
College Park, MD 20740
www.archives.gov

Recommended Reading

Following is a list of books that might be helpful in deciding whether a career in a mystery-related field is right for you. All are available from VGM Career Books.

Camenson, Blythe. *Careers in Writing.* 2000.
Camenson, Blythe. *Great Jobs for Anthropology Majors.* 1999.
Camenson, Blythe. *Opportunities in Forensic Science Careers.* 2001.
Coleman, Ronny J. *Opportunities in Fire Protection Careers,* Revised Edition. 2003.
DeGalan, Julie. *Great Jobs for Psychology Majors,* Second Edition. 2000.
DeGalan, Julie, and Stephen E. Lambert. *Great Jobs for History Majors,* Second Edition. 2001.
De la Pena, Kathleen, and Margaret Myers. *Opportunities in Library and Information Science.* 2001.
Dickel, Margaret Riley, and Frances E. Roehm. Guide to Internet Job Searching, 2002-2003. 2002.
Ferguson, Donald L., and Jim Patten. *Opportunities in Journalism Careers,* Revised Edition. 2001.
Goldberg, Jan. *Careers in Journalism,* Second Edition. 1999.
Lambert, Stephen E. *Great Jobs for Sociology Majors,* Second Edition. 2002.
Morgan, Marilyn. *Careers in Criminology.* 2000.

Munneke, Gary. *Careers in Law,* Third Edition. 2003.

Munneke, Gary, and Robert M. Greene. *Opportunities in Law Careers,* Revised Edition. 2001.

Regan, Debra, and Stephen E. Lambert. *Great Jobs for Criminal Justice Majors.* 2001.

Schwartz, Jerry. *Associated Press Reporting Handbook.* 2001.

Stinchcomb, James. *Opportunities in Law Enforcement and Criminal Justice Careers,* Second Edition. 2002.

About the Author

ver since she read her first Nancy Drew, Blythe Camenson has been a die-hard mystery fan. Combining that with her love of writing suspense novels and her position as director of Fiction Writer's Connection made this book a natural choice for her to write.

A full-time writer of career books, Blythe Camenson's main concern is helping job seekers make educated choices. She firmly believes that with enough information, readers can find long-term, satisfying careers. To that end she researches traditional as well as unusual occupations, talking to a variety of professionals about what their jobs are really like. In all of her books, she includes firsthand accounts from people who can reveal what to expect in each occupation.

Camenson was educated in Boston, earning her B.A. in English and psychology from the University of Massachusetts and her M.Ed. in counseling from Northeastern University.

In addition to *Careers for Mystery Buffs,* Camenson has written more than a dozen career guidance books for VGM Career Books.